THE ART OF JOURNALING

A COMPREHENSIVE GUIDE TO WRITING A JOURNAL

THE JOURNALING MASTERY SERIES: THEORY AND PRACTICE

BOOK 1

RICHARD FRENCH

Indie Pen Press

TURNING DREAMS INTO BESTSELLERS

Indie Pen Press
600 1st Ave Ste 330 PMB 582144
Seattle, Washington 98104-2246
IndiePenPress.com

Second Edition: October 2024

Paperback ISBN 979-8-9917570-1-0

🌸 Created with Vellum

INTRODUCTION

THE ART OF JOURNALING: A JOURNEY WITHIN

The blank page beckons, a world of possibilities unfolding before you. Your pen hovers, ready to capture the essence of your thoughts. Welcome to the art of journaling - a practice as old as writing itself, yet as fresh and relevant as your next breath.

Journaling is more than simply recording daily events. It's an intimate conversation with yourself, a canvas for exploration, and a mirror that reflects the deepest corners of your mind. Throughout history, profound thinkers, artists, and leaders have turned to their journals as a source of clarity, creativity, and self-discovery. Now it's your turn to join their ranks.

In The Art of Journaling: A Comprehensive Guide to Writing a Journal," you're invited to embark on a transformative journey. This book is your compass, guiding you through the vast landscape of personal writing. Whether you're a beginner picking up a journal for the first time or a seasoned writer looking to deepen your practice, these pages hold the key to unlocking new dimensions of your inner world.

At its core, journaling is about connection-a bridge that connects you to your thoughts, feelings, and the broader context of your life. It's a practice that fosters self-awareness and encourages you to explore your inner landscape with honesty and curiosity. Through regular journaling, you create a sacred space where you can safely process emotions, reflect on experiences, and gain insights that often remain hidden in the rush of daily life.

Imagine having a trusted confidant available at all times, day and night. Someone who listens without judgment, provides a space for reflection, and helps you make sense of your world. That's what your journal can be. It's a tool for self-discovery, revealing the patterns, desires, and fears that shape your actions and decisions. As you write, you may discover long-buried dreams or face challenges you've been avoiding.

In our increasingly fast-paced and demanding world, the simple act of putting pen to paper - or fingers to keyboard - can provide a much-needed refuge. Journaling provides a place to unburden the mind and find clarity in the midst of chaos. It's a powerful stress management tool that allows you to externalize your thoughts and feelings, making them more manageable and less overwhelming.

For those with a creative spirit, a journal is an infinite canvas, limited only by imagination. It's a playground where ideas can be born and nurtured without the constraints of judgment or criticism. Whether you're a writer, artist, musician, or simply someone who enjoys creative expression, your journal can be the incubator for your next great creation.

In addition to fostering creativity, journaling can also be a profound practice of mindfulness. In a world of constant distraction, taking time each day to journal helps you slow down and be present. This mindful approach allows you to reflect on your experiences with greater awareness, cultivating gratitude and a deeper connection to the present moment.

But where do you start? How do you transform the blank page from an intimidating void into a trusted friend? "The Art of Journaling guides you step-by-step through this process. You'll learn to identify your personal goals and intentions for journaling, explore different types of journals, and choose the right tools for your practice.

The book introduces different journaling methods, from stream-of-consciousness writing to structured reflection exercises. You'll discover techniques for overcoming writer's block and be reassured that there are no rules to journaling - only what works best for you. The book emphasizes that perfectionism has no place in your journal. Your entries don't have to be polished or profound; they simply have to be authentic.

As you progress through your journaling journey, you'll learn about gratitude journaling, which can help you focus on the positive aspects of life, and goal journaling, which can help you clarify and achieve your goals. There are sections on art journaling for those who prefer to express themselves visually, and travel journaling for capturing the essence of your adventures.

One of the most powerful aspects of journaling is its ability to track your personal growth over time. As you write consistently, you create a record of your thoughts, feelings, and experiences. Looking back at past entries can provide valuable insight into how far you've come, patterns you've overcome, and goals you've achieved.

Ultimately, The Art of Journaling is more than a guide-it's an invitation to embark on a journey of self-discovery and personal growth. By aligning your journaling practice with your personal goals, choosing the right tools, creating a supportive environment, and embracing the freedom to express yourself without judgment, you can unlock the full potential of this timeless art form.

So, are you ready to get started? Your journal awaits, a faithful companion on life's winding path. Open its pages, pick up your pen, and take the first step on this transformative journey. Who knows what insights, creations, or revelations await you? The only way to find out is to start writing. Your story begins now.

ONE
THE PURPOSE OF JOURNALING

1.1 UNDERSTANDING THE WHY

W hy do people keep journals?

From the private diaries of great historical figures to the artistic notebooks of artists and writers, people have been journaling for centuries. But why do people actually want to spend their precious time journaling? The reasons are as varied as the people who keep them. Some do it as a way of recording their daily lives and preserving their memories in amber. Others do it therapeutically to process emotions, work through problems, and clear their minds of clutter.

People keep journals for many reasons, not the least of which is self-discovery. A journal puts your thoughts and feelings in order; the information helps you understand your needs. Putting thoughts on paper often brings one's behavior into focus, exposes one's desires, and confronts one's fears. This habit can be very helpful for self-awareness and further personal growth over time.

Regular journaling is also a powerful technique for releasing accumulated stress. Surprisingly, writing is also a very cathartic exercise. You can release pent-up emotions and stress by venting through your writing. When overwhelmed, putting words to thoughts helps you organize your feelings and find a way out of the situation. It is a stress reliever and a method of maintaining mental health.

If you are a creative person, journaling is your canvas for creativity. Whether writing, sketching, or collaging, it is a place where you can develop ideas without fear of judgment, or a space where you can experiment with new concepts or record inspiration to develop your creative voice.

In addition, journaling can be used as a mindfulness practice. When the world rushes by, journaling each day is a way to take a moment to slow down and just be. As such, it provides an opportunity to reflect on your experiences, build gratitude, and connect with yourself. These mindful ways will increase overall feelings of peace and contentment.

Psychological and emotional reasons for journaling

The psychological and emotional benefits of journaling have been documented in numerous studies. As a form of self-help for emotional turmoil, ongoing journaling provides better mental health by providing a more organized way of processing emotions. For example, symptoms of depression and anxiety are reduced when a person writes about traumatic or stressful events. It works by externalizing thoughts and feelings, making them more understandable and manageable.

Journaling also allows you to understand your feelings in a much deeper way. You build a stronger connection to your feelings by constantly checking in with yourself through the pen. What you feel and why-knowing this emotional intelligence-will guide your relationships, your decisions, and your overall quality of life.

In other words, in addition to helping you manage your emotions, journaling can improve your problem-solving skills. Writing out problems or dilemmas provides a space to brainstorm solutions and look at the situation from different angles. This can lead to insights and solutions that you wouldn't have found otherwise.

JOURNALING FOR MINDFULNESS AND MENTAL CLARITY

Mindfulness is the practice of always being with what is right now, and journaling can be a really powerful way to develop this state of awareness. In mindful journaling, you pay attention only to writing: to the movement of the pen, to the flow of your thoughts, and to the emotions that are stirred. This practice not only improves your writing, but also quiets your mind and reduces all the chatter in your mind that leads to stress and anxiety.

In addition, journaling allows for mental clarity: one can untangle complex thoughts and emotions. When the going gets tough, writing can straighten it out, clarify the options at hand, and let you see which one is better to pursue based on your values. It's like having a conversation with yourself, where you can be completely honest and open.

1.2 PERSONAL GOAL IDENTIFICATION

Set intentions: What do you want to accomplish with your journal?

Remember to set your intentions beforehand for what you want to get out of journaling. This will give your journaling purpose and direction. Why do I want to journal? What do I want to explore or achieve? The answers will guide your approach to journaling and support your continued motivation.

Common journaling goals include:

- **Self-discovery**: Who you are and what you want out of life.
- **Emotional release**: Processing and releasing difficult feelings.
- **Personal development**: Realizing a new habit, skill, or perspective within yourself.

- **Creativity**: Exploring new ideas and expressing yourself artistically.
- **Goal Setting**: Planning and tracking personal or professional goals.

Once you know what your goals are, you can tailor your journaling practice to meet them. For example, if you are interested in self-discovery, you might focus most of your journaling on reflective prompts that encourage deep thinking. If your goal is to inspire creativity, you might use your journal as a place to brainstorm and sketch ideas.

Different types of journals

There are countless types of journals, each designed to serve a different purpose. Some of the most popular include:

- **Personal Diary**: This type is a daily account of what you feel, think, and experience. Most often, reflection or emotional processing is appropriate for entries.
- **Dream journal**: A log of your dreams, used to explore your subconscious and gain insight into your waking life.
- **Bullet Journal**: An organizational system that is highly customizable, integrating one's tasks, habits, and even goals.
- **Gratitude Journal:** A type of journal that requires you to write about what you are grateful for each day, boosting your mood and increasing your happiness.
- **Creative Journal**: This is the area where creativity is unleashed through writing, drawing, painting, and collage.
- **Travel Journal**: A record of your travels, including descriptions of places visited, people met, and experiences.
- **Health Journal**: Keeping a journal of your physical and mental health, including symptoms, diet, nutrition, exercise, and moods.
- **Prayer or Meditation Journal**: Space to document your prayer or spiritual reflections and meditations.

Aligning Your Journaling Practice with Your Life Goals To take your journaling a little deeper, you may want to keep it integrated with the bigger picture of your life goals. For example, if you are practicing growth on a personal level, this journal will help you set and track your goals, reflect on your progress to date, and identify areas for improvement. If you are focusing on creativity, your journal can be a place to experiment with new ideas and track your creative journey. How journaling can work with your goals: For example, do you want to incorporate a new habit, exercise, or meditation into your life? Your journal can measure your progress and serve as a reminder to keep up the pace. Are you having a difficult time in your life? Journaling can help you process your emotions in a clear way. In this way, journaling can continue to be meaningful and valuable in your daily life. The journal will take on a whole new meaning for you: not just notes on paper, but a tool to help you create the life you want.

CONCLUSION

The goals and objectives of journaling can vary greatly from person to person. Whether it's finding yourself, expressing your emotions, being creative, or simply organizing your thoughts, journaling fits into any lifestyle and is a flexible and powerful tool for personal growth. What you write in your journal is determined by your personal needs and goals, your understanding of what motivates you, and your clear intentions, so that it becomes a meaningful, life-changing way to journal.

TWO
GETTING STARTED

2.1 CHOOSING THE RIGHT TOOLS

S electing the Right Journal

With journaling, it all starts with the journal itself. Simply put, the right journal can serve as an inspiration for writing, while the wrong one-yes, you guessed it-will become an obstacle. But with so many options, how do you choose the one that's right for you?

First, let's look at the size factor. Maybe you want it small and portable enough to take with you everywhere, or maybe you prefer larger books that give you more room to write. Perhaps a pocket-sized journal would be fine for jotting down quick thoughts on the go; if you want to write something more substantial or even do some creative work, an A5 or letter-sized notebook might be appropriate.

Next, consider the quality of the paper. If you like to write with a fountain pen or in mixed media - watercolors or markers - a journal with thicker, high-quality paper is a must to avoid bleeding or tearing. On the other hand, if you only use a ballpoint pen or your style is very minimal, you may be able to get away with a plain notebook.

Another important factor is the binding of the journal. A journal that lies flat when opened can make writing more comfortable if you will be writing in it for a very long time. Spiral-bound journals allow for easier page turning and can be folded back on themselves, which is handy when writing in tight spaces.

Finally, there is the issue of format: some people like lined pages that are structured for writing, or sometimes they appreciate the freedom of blank pages that allow them to draw and sketch. There are even dot grid and graph paper options, ideal for bullet journaling or more technical layouts.

PEN OR DIGITAL? THE PROS AND CONS

In today's digital world, journaling is not limited to paper or any other type of journal. Many people find online journaling just as effective, if not more so, with the convenience and flexibility it offers. Here is a quick look at the pros and cons of both:

PAPER JOURNALING

Paper Journaling Pros

- **Tactile experience**: Journaling by hand is even more personal and reflective; it helps with the ability to connect more deeply with your thoughts.
- **Creativity**: Paper journals allow for a lot of creativity through doodling, collaging, or using different colors and materials.
- **No distractions**: A paper journal doesn't have the notifications and Internet that come with digital devices.
- **Physical record**: It is very nice to have a physical book that you can hold and look at for memory's sake.
- Disadvantages
- **Portability**: While small journals could be portable, they would remain bulky compared to a phone or tablet.

- **Space**: Once you fill up a journal, you have to find a place to store it, which can take up physical space.
- **No backup**: Your entries may be irretrievable if your journal is lost or destroyed.

Digital Journaling

Pros

- **Convenience**: You can log journal entries from anywhere in the world, at any time, using a smartphone, tablet, or computer.
- **Searchability**: Digital journals are easily searchable, making it easy to find entries or topics by typing in keywords.
- **Multimedia**: You can easily include photos, videos, and links in your posts.
- **Security**: Digital journals can be password-protected and backed up to minimize the risk of loss.

Disadvantages

- **Distractions**: Overall, digital devices are full of distractions that can get in the way of writing in your journal.
- **More impersonal**: For some, typing just doesn't have the emotional feel of handwriting.
- **Too dependent on technology**: Of course, digital journaling requires some form of device with a power source.

Paper and digital journaling is really just a matter of personal preference. Some may even have a hybrid system where they get the best of both worlds. For example, you might keep a traditional paper journal for reflective writing, but also keep a digital app for quick notes or goal tracking.

CREATE SPACE TO JOURNAL

Where you journal can be just as important as how you journal. Creating a space specifically for journaling can further your goal of creating a habit and even making it an enjoyable activity. And it doesn't have to be anything fancy-just a comfortable, inviting space free of distractions.

Here are some tips for setting up your journaling space:

- **Find a quiet place**: Find a place where no one will disturb you. It could be a corner of your room, a comfortable chair in your living room, or even outside in nature.
- **Make it comfortable**: Have a comfortable chair and something to write on. You will want good lighting, either natural light from a window or a well-placed lamp.
- **Make the space your own**: Have things around you that inspire you, such as plants, artwork, or photos. You may also want to keep your favorite pen, marker, or other journaling tools close by.
- **Minimize distractions**: Try to fill your journaling space with minimal clutter and far fewer distractions. Turn off your phone, close your laptop, and focus on what you are doing - writing.

By creating an environment that is truly conducive to reflection and creation, you will easily get into your journaling mindset and use it to your advantage.

2.2 OVERCOMING THE BLANK PAGE

Getting Started Tips

The biggest barrier to journaling is often knowing how to start with what is typically a blank page. A blank page is daunting, especially if it is new to you or if you feel stuck in some way. Fortunately, there are several strategies you can use to get your thoughts flowing.

Prompt: The whole idea of writing prompts is to spark the creativity of great ideas. A prompt can be a helpful question, quote, or simple statement that gets you thinking and then writing. For example, it could be something like, "What am I thankful for today?" or "Describe a recent challenge and how you overcame it.

Free writing involves setting a timer for 5-10 minutes and just writing without stopping. Do not worry about grammar, spelling, or making sense; just let your thoughts flow. This exercise can disregard your inner critic and allow you to just get your ideas down on paper.

Keep lists: Lists are an easy and organized way to get started writing. You can list anything - your goals, things you love, places you'd like to visit, books you'd like to read, etc. Lists can be a fun, less daunting way to begin your journaling.

Use visual aids: When the words don't come, it's best to start with a drawing, doodle, or collage. Sometimes a visual can release the creative juices and turn into something that your writing can then expand upon.

Start with a question: This can be one of the most powerful ways to start a journal entry. It can be introspective-"How am I feeling right now?" or "What am I trying to do today?"-and the answer develops both a starting point and a direction.

Overcoming Writer's Block

All of the blockers described above will affect every writer at some point, and journalists are not exempt. The trick to overcoming writer's block is to recognize it for what it is: temporary - but not a problem that will necessarily stop you from journaling.

Here are some techniques to help you get through it:

- **Get a change of scenery**: Sometimes change can spark creativity. If you're used to journaling at home, try journaling at a diner, a park, or the library.
- **Write about the block**: If you are completely at a loss, try writing about being at a loss. Describe the frustration, struggle with the idea of what is blocking you, and see where it takes you.
- **Set small goals**: Instead of putting pressure on yourself to write a lot, set your goal for the day to write just one sentence or even one word. Sometimes that small step allows you to break through the block.
- **Engage your senses**: Take a moment to look around you-the colors and sensations you pick up, the smells, the tastes, and the feels. Writing about these things will engage your senses and stimulate more words on the page.
- **Don't force it**: If this is really hard for you, it is okay to take a break. Journaling is meant to be positive, not a chore. Give yourself permission to step away and return when you're feeling more inspired.

UNDERSTAND THAT THERE ARE NO RULES

One of the most liberating things about journaling is that there are no real rules. Your journal is yours to use as you see fit. This means that spelling, grammar, and whether what you have written is "good enough" are not things you need to worry about. You don't have to write in a certain format, every day, or according to some outsider's rules. If you want to write a single word on the page or fill pages with reflections, that's fine. If you want to skip days, or mix journaling methods, or use it for doodling versus writing, that is perfectly fine. The idea behind journaling is to create an element of practice that serves your needs and brings you joy. Let your journal be a form of expression, development, and exploration for you. This is a place where you can be completely honest, play with ideas, and ponder your thoughts without judgment. Embrace the freedom of journaling and let your writing be the way that comes naturally and is fulfilling to you.

CONCLUSION

Getting started with journaling is a matter of finding the right tools, creating the right space, and overcoming the initial problems associated with the blank page. You can set yourself up for success and create a rewarding, sustainable journaling practice by choosing a journal that fits your style, creating a comfortable writing environment, and allowing yourself the freedom to write without rules. As you begin to explore this process, it is important to remember that the most important thing about journaling is that it reflects your unique voice and meets your personal needs.

THREE
JOURNALING TECHNIQUES

3.1 KEEPING A JOURNAL

B UILD HABITS: ESTABLISHING A ROUTINE
One of the ways to effectively incorporate journaling into your life is to make it part of your daily habit system. As with any habit, the key is consistency. The practice of daily journaling has built momentum in my life; over time, it has truly become part of my routine. As one gradually reflects, processes, and documents thoughts and experiences on a regular basis, the benefits of daily journaling begin to accrue.

To help you establish your daily journaling habit, consider the following tips:

- **Set the time**: It is important to choose a time of day that is more convenient for you-whether it is first thing in the morning, around lunchtime, or before bed. You will have established your routine so that journaling becomes part of your daily life.

- **Start small**: Since this is your first experience with daily journaling, you should take a small amount of time. You do not need to write pages and pages; sometimes a short entry is powerful. Over time, as you gain confidence, you can gradually increase your journaling.
- **Cue a response**: Associate journaling with a well-learned daily activity, such as drinking your first cup of coffee in the morning or relaxing before bed. This previously learned action will then serve as a cue to journaling and will help the practice become an ingrained part of your routine.
- **Be flexible**: Consistency is important, but don't be too hard on yourself. Life sometimes takes an unusual turn that may leave you without enough time to make your journal entry for the day. This is okay; the trick is to get back on track as soon as possible, without guilt or pressure.
- **Celebrate your progress**: Feel good about the fact that you are still committed and that you have gone through the exercise of journaling. Celebrate milestones, such as completing your first week or month of daily journaling. This kind of positive reinforcement can motivate you to keep going.
- **Morning pages**: Do this as soon as you wake up. The concept of morning pages is a journaling technique developed by Julia Cameron in her book The Artist's Way: as soon as you wake up in the morning, write three longhand, stream-of-consciousness pages. The goal is not to come up with a beautiful piece of prose, polished to perfection, but to get all the clutter out of your head and set a positive tone for the rest of the day.

LET'S START WITH MORNING PAGES

Morning pages work best because you can write down all your fears and negative thoughts that may be clouding your mind. One would write them down first thing in the morning so that they can be cleared from the mental noise. This also helps to stimulate one's creativity because there's a little bit of processing and therefore one can follow what's in one's heart and come up with something new.

Writing in the morning allows you to capture your thoughts before the day's distractions get in the way. Writing in the morning taps into your subconscious and your thoughts flow.

- **Don't overthink it**: Morning pages should be raw and unfiltered. Forget about grammar, spelling, or even making sense. Just let your thoughts flow onto the paper.
- **Commit to three pages**: The guideline behind three pages is to get you past the initial resistance and into deeper layers of thought. From those three pages, things will continue to expand and take shape.
- **Keep it private**: The Morning Pages are for your eyes only. You can be completely raw and honest, knowing that no one else will ever read them.

EVENING REFLECTION

Review your day and plan for the day ahead.

Evening pages help you clear your mind of worries before you go to sleep. Again, simply review the day-what worked, where your challenges were, and what you learned. And maybe even what you want to do tomorrow.

Evening reflections can also be used to get a better night's sleep; to release any lingering anxiety and stress. Put them to rest by writing down your thoughts and perhaps bringing some closure to the day.

I practice evening reflections by:

- **Recapitulating your day**: Write down the highlights of what actually happened during the day. Note the events and successes, along with anything you may have found challenging.

- **Reflect on your feelings**: Think about your mood throughout the day; were there moments when you were happy, frustrated, or anxious? What made you feel those emotions and how did you respond?
- **Celebrate your victories**: Recognize what you've done well - no matter how small the victory - with a round of applause. Celebrating your success helps reinforce positive behavior and gives you confidence.
- **Identify areas for improvement**: Reflect on the challenging moments and failures. What would you have done differently and how will you approach a similar situation in the future?
- **Set intentions for tomorrow:** Complete your reflection by looking forward to the next day. What needs to be accomplished? What do you want to bring into tomorrow's mindset? Setting intentions prepares you to approach the next day with focus and purpose.

3.2 CREATIVE JOURNALING

Merge words with art: Sketches, Collages, Mixed Media

Creative journaling uses more than just words; it includes sketches, collages, and mixed media. This could be a really good fit for someone who loves to express art, or someone who wants to develop their ideas in a non-linear way.

In an art journal, you could combine writing with:

- **Sketches and drawings**: You can include visual cues from your current thoughts or experiences that help give your journal a little more depth. You don't have to be a fine artist, even doodles or abstract shapes would do wonders.
- **Collages**: Find and paste images from your magazines,

newspapers, or other cutting sources to create visual stories or mood boards to accompany your writing.

- **Mixed Media**: Add new dimensions to your journal pages with materials as diverse as fabric, paint, or washi tape to make them more enticing and engaging.
- **Lettering and calligraphy**: You can include different fonts, lettering styles, or even calligraphy in your journal; it can really add a personal touch to some important quotes or affirmations.

Creative journaling encourages you to look beyond the usual ways of expressing yourself. It helps you find a new way to express yourself, and most importantly, it is a free and playful way of journaling that rekindles your love for it.

STREAM OF CONSCIOUSNESS WRITING: JUST LET THE IDEAS FLOW

Stream-of-consciousness writing is the free-writing process of not lifting the pen from the page as you put words on paper. It tries to put down the natural mind and let any thoughts come up on their own. The way to get to those feelings, thoughts, or deeper ideas would be through structured writing.

Go Practice Writing Stream of Consciousness

Use a timer: 5 minutes, 10 minutes - and just write nonstop until it goes off. This will help you overcome past resistance and dive into your subconscious.

- **Write without judgment**: There is no concern about whether a point makes sense, is coherent, or even uses the rules of grammar. The idea is to write whatever comes to mind, no matter how random or unrelated it may seem.
- **Keep going**: If you get stuck, just write "I don't know what to write" until a new thought comes. The writing itself will eventually lead you to new ideas.

- **Review Later (Optional)** : After you've written a significant number of Flow of Consciousness entries, you might want to go back and see if there are any patterns, insights, or ideas that emerge naturally from all those entries. This isn't necessary, of course, and sometimes the act of writing is what's important.

Freewriting in a stream of consciousness is so freeing because it allows you to explore your thoughts in a raw and unfiltered way, bypassing the inner critic. It can also be very helpful in finding a new perspective or breaking through writer's block.

Poetry and Prose: Writing and Discovery Through Journaling

The journal should be large enough to accommodate a little creativity; poetry, prose, and the like. This is the most artistic and imaginative way to explore emotions, ideas, and stories. Whether you are an experienced writer or just experimenting, using your journal for creative writing can be fun and rewarding.

Writing Poetry

- **Free verse**: Try writing poetry without the restrictions of rhyme or meter. Free verse allows you to focus on imagery, feeling, and the way language flows in nature.
- **Prompts**: Let prompts inspire your poetry. For example: Write a poem about a specific memory, feeling, or moment in nature.
- **Form and Structure**: Experiment with different poetic forms. Haikus, sonnets, acrostics, and more. Structure can be a fun creative problem or just another way to push your work further.

Writing Prose

- **Short stories**: Develop short stories based on your past experiences or invented situations. Journaling is a really safe space to explore new ideas and characters.

- **Descriptive writing**: Aim for descriptive prose that captures details of a place, person, scene, or event. This can help develop skills in creating imagery through writing.
- **Character sketches**: Write about the people in your life or create new characters. Describe their appearance, personality, and backstory. This can actually be quite fun and helps you get a different perspective.

Being able to write both poetry and prose in my journal gives me a chance to tap into my creative side and explore languages in new and exciting ways. It's a nice way to express myself and improve my writing skills.

3.3 THEMES

Gratitude journaling: Focusing on the good things in life

Gratitude journaling is an intentional practice in which you regularly write about the things for which you are grateful. By noticing the good things in life and the reasons for gratitude, gratitude journaling can improve mood, contribute to an enhanced sense of well-being, and shift a negative outlook to one of optimism.

BEGIN A GRATITUDE JOURNAL

Keep a daily list, and at the end of the day, write down three to five things you have had the opportunity to be grateful for. Things can range from the mundane, such as a meaningful conversation with a friend, to the extraordinary, such as a gourmet meal.

- **Be specific**: Instead of general statements such as "I am grateful for my family," try to personalize or be more specific.

For example, "I am grateful for the way my sister made me laugh today.

- **Why reflect**: Reflecting on why you are thankful for each thing increases your sense of gratitude and helps you appreciate the impact these things have on your life.
- **Do it on tough days**: Whenever you are down and having a rough day, go back through some of your gratitude journal entries. Reading what you have been grateful for over time might just lift your spirits and bring some good vibes into your life.

Gratitude journaling is one of those very simple yet profound practices that can really change the way you look at life. By regularly practicing what you're grateful for, you train your brain to focus on the positive, which generally produces more happiness and contentment.

GOAL SETTING JOURNALS: TRACK PROGRESS AND SUCCESS

Goal journals allow you to achieve goals in your personal or professional life by writing them down and reviewing them regularly. It keeps you accountable and motivated to achieve your goal.

To create a goal journal

- **Define your goals**: Start by writing down your long-term and short-term goals. Be very specific, and remember to make sure they meet the SMART criterion, which ensures that your goals are clear and attainable: Specific, Measurable, Achievable, Relevant, Time-Bound.
- **Break it down**: For each goal, break it down into smaller, more manageable pieces or milestones. These big goals will not seem overwhelming if you take them one step at a time, and you will have a clear plan for how to achieve them.
- **Track your progress**: Update your progress regularly in your journal. Make notes about successes, difficulties, and changes

you may want to make. This will keep you on track and show you how far you have come.

- **Reflect and review**: At any time, reflect on your goals and consider what is working and what is not. Do not be afraid to make changes to your goals and ways of achieving them; a lot of flexibility is needed to stay motivated and adaptable at the same time.

A Goal Setting Journal - a powerful tool for achieving your dreams. By writing down your goals and reviewing them over and over again, you are sure to achieve them.

DREAM JOURNALS: WRITING AND INTERPRETING YOUR DREAMS

Dream journals contain the content of your dreams and are used to explore them. They usually contain symbols and scenarios that provide a good insight into a person's subconscious. In this way, dream journals provide a starting point for reading the hidden messages of one's dreams for personal growth.

Starting a Dream Journal

- **Keep it by your bed**: Have you kept your journal and pen close to your bed so that you can write down your dreams as soon as you wake up? Dreams are usually very fleeting, so it is important to record them before they disappear.
- **Record them immediately**: When you wake up, write down everything you can remember about your dream. This includes details about the setting, the characters, the emotions surrounding the dream, and any symbols or special events that stood out.
- **Reflect on the meanings**: After recording, take a few moments to reflect on what your dream meant. How did it make you feel? Does it relate to anything in your physical life? What might the symbols be trying to represent?

- **Look for patterns**: From time to time, go back and read your dream journal to look for repeated themes, symbols or emotions. These patterns can convey many messages from your subconscious about personal growth.

Dream journaling is a fascinating practice that can deepen your understanding of yourself and your inner world. By exploring your dreams, you become aware of the hidden components of your psyche, and this knowledge can be used to improve your waking life.

CONCLUSION

There are almost as many ways to write in a journal as there are people who keep journals. Whether it is organizing daily routines, getting creative with an artistic outlet, or delving into a themed journal, there is a technique to help you meet your own particular needs and goals. You can work with these different approaches and find the kind of journaling that works best for you, making the practice both meaningful and enjoyable. Each technique offers a different way to engage with your thoughts, process your emotions, and document your journey, making journaling a versatile and powerful tool for personal growth.

FOUR
DEEPENING YOUR PRACTICE

4.1 REFLECTIVE JOURNAL

Asking Deeper Questions Exploring Your Thoughts

Reflective journaling is a powerful way to explore your thoughts and feelings on a much deeper level. Unlike conclusion-oriented journal entries that simply recount events or observations of the day, reflective journaling asks many questions and seeks reasons for events and reactions. Such reflection will bring into focus one's beliefs, motivations, and current behavior, thus developing self-awareness and personal growth.

Beginning with the following practices can lead a student into reflective journaling:

When describing an event or feeling in a journal, ask yourself "why" several times. For example, "**I feel anxious, why?**" Then, after the answer, ask, "**Why does this make me anxious?**" Keep doing this until you get to what you really mean.

Use prompts: Reflective prompts can help you direct your writing to bring out important insights. For example:

- **"What did I gain from this?"**
- **"How did I contribute to this situation?"**
- **"What do I need to believe in order to act in this way?**
- **"How do I want to grow from this?"**

Challenge your assumptions: Reflective journaling is the time when you may want to look for these assumptions and beliefs. Try to see why you feel that way and whether those views serve you. For example, suppose you believe that success is about perfection. Ask yourself how this belief has affected your life and whether it's realistic or helpful.

Vary your perspective: Try to discover the different possible ways of describing the situation. For example, how would someone else make sense of what is happening to me? How would my future self reflect on this moment? This keeps you challenged and sensitive to other possibilities in a very helpful way.

Reflective journaling is a practice that will be transformative, leading to deep realizations and self-development. It asks you to go a little deeper, just to challenge you, thus creating a space for growth and self-discovery.

Analyzing patterns: Recognizing Recurring Themes in Your Writing

One of the richest qualities of reflective journaling is the ability to recognize patterns in thoughts, behaviors, and feelings over time. As you write and read regularly in your journal, recurring themes or even a pattern may emerge in your daily life. These provide a glimpse of a place where one may be stuck, recurring issues, or consistent beliefs that continue to shape experiences.

You can find patterns in your journaling by:

- **Reviewing regularly**: Set aside some time-perhaps once a month or quarterly-to go over your journal entries.

Sometimes certain words, phrases, emotions, or situations seem to recur. They may be telling you what is on your mind or influencing your behavior.

- **Highlight or categorize them**: Read through your journal. Identify themes that you discuss the most or that recur. For example, you may notice that these are things that cause you stress at work, or that you really do think about relationships all the time. Categorizing them allows you to see how often and under what circumstances they occur.

- **Reflect on the meaning**: Once you find patterns, think about what they mean. Why do these themes recur? Are they unresolved issues or areas of your life that need to be explored? Recognizing the meaning behind these patterns can guide your future actions and decisions.

- **Track progress**: Pattern analysis also allows you to track progress over time. For example, if you have been working on improving your self-confidence, rereading your journal can show how your thoughts and behaviors have changed. This is incredibly motivating and validating.

If you can identify and reflect on patterns in your journaling, you are likely to gain a better understanding of yourself, and you may also discover ways in which you need to grow. As these patterns are brought to light, you are empowered to choose what to do about them.

Journaling as therapy: Using Your Journal to Work Through Issues

You can work through the most difficult emotions, learn to cope with the toughest times, and gain insight into the most painful feelings by journaling. While journaling is not professional therapy, it can complement such therapeutic work and provide a safe space for self-expression and healing.

JOURNALING AS A THERAPEUTIC TOOL

- **Write about your feelings**: When dealing with overwhelming emotions, the act of writing is seen as a way to process and vent. Don't let go; allow yourself to fully express what you're feeling, whether it's anger, sadness, fear, or joy. Writing can be cathartic and bring clarity.
- **Identify your triggers**: Writing in a journal can help you discover what kinds of situations, people, or thoughts tend to make you feel wildly emotional. By exploring these triggers in your journal, you can begin to uncover their origins and find ways to deal with them.
- **Self-Compassion**: The journal can become an ideal place to practice self-compassion, especially during difficult times. Write to yourself as you would to a friend, with kindness and empathy. Acknowledge the struggle without judgment and remind yourself that your feelings are okay.
- **Reframe negative thoughts**: If you find yourself stuck in negative thought patterns, use your journal to challenge and reframe them. For example, if you write, "I always mess up," follow up with, "What evidence do I have that this is true? What are some examples of times when I have been successful?" Reframing helps you shift your perspective and gain a more balanced view.
- **Set intentions for your healing**: Journaling can also be an opportunity to set intentions for your healing journey. You can write about what you need to heal from, what steps you can take, and how you want to feel in the future. Setting these intentions gives you direction and purpose.

As a therapeutic tool, journaling helps you channel your emotions in a constructive way. It can lift a weight from your shoulders, provide insight into a challenge, or support your own being.

4.2 LONG-TERM JOURNALING

Revisiting Old Journals - Learning from Your Past Self

One of the most satisfying aspects of long-term journaling is the ability to revisit entries from long ago. Rereading past entries allows you to reflect on how much you have grown, remember lessons learned, and look at many of life's old challenges with fresh eyes. Savings from decisions made by your past self will come to mind when you have forgotten or overlooked them.

To get the most out of revisiting old journal entries:

- **Set a time frame**: You can then focus on entries written within certain time frames of your life - a difficult year, a time of transition, a year of growth... This way you can see how you have evolved and what has changed.
- **Look for growth**: As you read through some of your past entries, notice how your thoughts, beliefs, and feelings have subtly changed over time. Applaud your growth and look at the progress you have made, even if it feels small.
- **Reflect on difficult experiences you have had in the past**: Read through entries where you wrote about difficult experiences. How did you deal with the challenge at that time? What did you take away from it? These moments of reflection will give you insight into your resilience and the strategies that helped you simply get through the obstacles.
- **New insights**: Re-reading old entries, especially about key dates/events, may provide some new insights into the present. You may recognize patterns or themes that you are still dealing with, or you may see a past experience in a new light. Use these insights to inform your present decisions and actions.
- **Be kind to your past self**: Read the past entries aloud and be kind to your former self. You may cringe at certain thoughts or decisions, but remember that you did the best you could

with the knowledge and resources you had at the time. Be gentle with yourself.

One of the most powerful ways to touch your past and learn from your experiences is to revisit old journal entries. Of course, it can also increase self-awareness, as sometimes very good life lessons can be brought out that can eventually be carried well into the present.

Journaling Over the Years: How Your Practice Can Evolve Over Time

As you grow and change, so will your journaling practice. What works for you today may not be the same as what worked for you a year ago, and that's okay. Journaling is an ever-evolving process: it shifts with each new development to meet the needs, interests, and goals you're working toward.

Here are some ways your journaling practice might change and evolve over time:

- **Shifts in focus**: It is likely that your journaling focus will shift over time: for example, you may have started with reflections related to everyday life, but then shifted to goal setting, creative writing, or spiritual exploration. Allow your journaling practice to shift as your life does.
- **Format changes**: The format you prefer may also change. You may start with a traditional paper journal, then find yourself moving to a digital format, or vice versa. You may try different types of journals, such as bullet journals, art journals, or gratitude journals, depending on what works for you at the time.
- **Evolving themes**: The themes in your journals are likely to evolve over the course of your life. Early on, you may be preoccupied with career goals, but later you may be interested in themes of relationships, personal growth, or spirituality.
- **Develop a deeper practice**: Over time, your journaling practice may deepen. You may move from surface-level

reflections to deeper explorations of your inner world. You may feel that it becomes a bit more intentional as you go along; it grows more out of the practice of what might be considered self-awareness and mindfulness, let's say, personal development.

- **Incorporating new techniques**: Over time, you may find yourself wanting to use new techniques, such as reflective journaling, stream-of-consciousness writing, or creative journaling. Trying new methods can refresh your practice and keep it interesting.

The fact is that it is a reflection of life and, as such, can hardly remain static for long. You'll want to embrace these changes and let your journal grow with you, which is often helped by a new focus.

Archiving Life Milestones: Turning Your Journal into a Life Archive

One of the most meaningful elements of journaling can be using it to record life milestones and key experiences. A journal is your own archive, keeping a proper record of the events, decisions, and experiences that shape your life. Such an archive becomes a valuable resource for recalling important memories and reflecting on how far you've come.

To record life experiences in your journal:

- **Document key events**: These include major life events such as graduations, weddings, births, career changes, moves, etc. Note how the situation changed your thoughts and feelings and how it affected your life.
- **Capture everyday moments**: Not every moment will be extraordinary, but sometimes those are the ones that mean the most when you look back years later.
- **Photos and memorabilia can be included**: Consider including photos, tickets, letters, or other mementos that are important to you in your physical journal. All of these tangible

items can add another layer of depth to your life archive and make the experience a little more vivid.

- **Reflect on personal accomplishments**: Use your journal to celebrate personal accomplishments, no matter how small. From reaching a fitness goal, to completing a major project, to simply overcoming personal difficulties, record these moments in your journey as recognition and appreciation of growth.
- **Write letters to your future self from time to time**: This can be a great reflection of where you are now and where you want to be in the future. When you look back on these letters in a few years, it feels powerful to reflect on how far you have come and where life has taken you.

By recording life's milestones in your journal, you make it a repository of your personal history. This repository serves not only to preserve your memories, but also as a testament and witness to growth, resilience, and the experiences that have shaped your personality.

4.3 SHARING YOUR JOURNAL

Deciding whether or not to share your journal entries with others

Journaling is essentially an individual activity; however, there are times when you find it absolutely essential to express and share what you are going through with another person. Sharing your journal can be for the purpose of connecting with others, for feedback, or simply to give insight into your thoughts and experiences. However, the decision has to be personal, and one has to think carefully about sharing one's journal with someone.

Here are some things to consider when deciding whether to share your journal:

- **Purpose**: Why do you want to share your journal? If you're just looking for validation or connection, be honest about that. Understanding this can really help you understand whether or not you should share it.
- **Audience**: Think about who you might share your journal with; it could be a good friend, a family member, your therapist. Some audiences may react differently to your entries, so you need to think about who the person reading the journal would be.
- **Boundaries**: Set clear boundaries for what you are comfortable sharing. You do not have to share everything-just the entries that you feel comfortable discussing-and keep the rest private.
- **Impact**: Consider how sharing your journal will affect your relationship. Will it close a gap between you and the person you share with, or will it cause friction? Be sensitive to the potential consequences.
- **Timing**: Consider when it would be a good time to share your journal. Sometimes it is better to allow some time to pass so that you can help yourself process some of the thoughts and feelings before sharing them with others.

Sharing a journal is the condition that drives vulnerability, but it also helps to build broader relationships and understanding. If you choose to share, do so thoughtfully and in relation to your needs and limitations.

GROUP JOURNALING: SHARED REFLECTION, SHARED GROWTH

Group journaling involves coming together to write, share, and reflect on the experiences gained through journaling. This group approach is likely to provide the sense of community and support to shed new light on one's journaling experience. It can be used in a variety of settings, such as writing groups, therapy sessions, or workshops.

Some benefits of group journaling include

- **Shared experience**: Writing and sharing in a group allows you to participate in something that is fundamentally shared. It also allows you to connect feelings and experiences.
- **Different perspectives**: Listening to others' reflections can broaden your perspective on what has happened to you. Group members can provide feedback, encouragement, or different perspectives that facilitate the journaling process.
- **Accountability**: Group journaling is a self-regulating process. You will do your journaling on time, knowing that you will be sharing your work with others, so you will stay on schedule with your practice.
- **Facilitated growth**: In the process of group journaling, there are times when a guided prompt or discussion can help you find areas of self-reflection that are new to you. Often a facilitator will introduce you to new journaling techniques and topics that you would never have come across on your own.

If you're interested in group journaling, consider joining or starting a journaling group in your area or online. Many community organizations, writing centers, and online platforms offer opportunities for group journaling, so it's easy to give it a try. Group journaling can deepen your practice and make the journey less lonely by providing a powerful way to connect with others on the same journey - through one-time workshops or regular meetings.

Publishing Your Journal: From Personal Pages to Public Expression

For some people, the idea of exposing the contents of their journal to a public audience, as in publishing, can be both liberating and terrifying. Transforming your journal into a published work is just a process of making something so uncomfortable public, and therefore needs to be decided with care.

If you want your journal to be published:

- **Cherry-pick your entries**: Choose which parts of your journal you want to make public. Not every entry needs to be published; choose the ones that resonate most with your audience or tell a coherent story.
- **Edit for clarity**: Personal journal entries are raw and unfiltered, which is part of their appeal. When preparing your journal for publication, edit for clarity, coherence, and readability. This may mean expanding on certain ideas, providing some context, or removing parts that are overly personal or obscure.
- **Maintain originality**: Editing is important, but it is equally important that your voice in the journal still sound like you. Often, what draws people to read published journals is the openness and the fact that you are putting yourself out there. So try to maintain the original tone of your writing.
- **Consider the impact on yourself and others**: Think about how writing and later publishing your journal might affect your life and the lives of others who might be mentioned in your entries. Be sensitive to privacy issues and how others might feel about reading about you.
- **Choose your format**: There are so many ways to publish a journal. Everything from traditional print publishing to self-publishing on the Internet. Consider which format fits your goals and your audience. You might decide to publish a book, start a blog, or contribute excerpts to a literary magazine.

Publishing your journal can be a way to share your story with others, but also to join the larger conversation about issues that affect you. It is a chance to turn your personal thoughts into something public that can inspire and touch readers who may see themselves in those words.

CONCLUSION

You are moving toward a deeper engagement with the practice of journaling by looking at newer techniques, considering growth, and how to share your experiences with others. In other words, you may be looking at reflective journaling, re-reading entries written at a different time in your life-and perhaps considering publication. Each step adds layers of meaning and insight to your journaling. Allow yourself to change, to experiment, and to engage with the larger community of journalers. Be sure to engage in your journey. Through this process, you will see how your journal has become something more than a record of your life. That it is truly a powerful tool for transformation and self-discovery.

FIVE
ADVANCED JOURNALING CONCEPTS

5.1 INTEGRATING TECHNOLOGY

APPS FOR DIGITAL JOURNALING: A MODERN WRITER'S AID.
The art of journaling in the digital world is done without pen and paper. The many supporting features make up the digital and journaling apps that make the process both easy and limitless. Most of these apps do everything from simple note-taking to elaborate life tracking.

Below are some notable digital journaling applications and their features:

Day One was once the poster child for what digital journaling applications could be. It presents a clean, intuitive interface. Features include automatic metadata (including weather and location), the ability to attach photos and videos, and end-to-end encryption for privacy. It also supports multiple journals, tagging, and search capabilities, making managing and searching an archive quite intuitive.

Travel: This app allows you to do just about anything with your journal - daily prompts, mood tracking, and backup to Google Drive if you'd like. Journey also has a web version, so you can access your journal from any device.

Penzu: Offers strong privacy protection with military-grade encryption to protect entries. A user can customize covers, insert images, and email entries to your inbox or anyone else's in the application.

Concept: Not really a journaling app, but the sheer power of Notion makes it perfect for digital journaling. You can create your own custom digital journal using templates, add images and links, and organize entries using databases and tags.

Microsoft OneNote: Offers a freer form of journaling than any of its competitors. It allows you to create many notebooks with free sections and pages, which means you can have a document where you can write, draw, and insert anything in any format. This solution satisfies both structured journaling needs and creative free-form journaling.

BENEFITS OF DIGITAL JOURNALING

Accessibility: You can access your entries from any device with digital journaling, making it convenient to keep the process going while you lead a mobile life.

Searchability: Digital journals are searchable, facilitating the possibility to search for entries, keywords, or themes.

Multimedia integration: You can easily add photos, videos, voice recordings, and links to your entries, enhancing your journaling experience.

Safety: Most applications include this feature, which includes all types, such as encryption, password protection, and all others, making sure your private thoughts are well kept.

Automatic backups: Digital journals are capable of being automatically backed up into cloud-based solutions thereby minimizing losses.

DIGITAL JOURNALING CONS

Distractions: It is undeniably easy to be tempted into distractions via notifications or opening other apps when trying to write on a digital device.

Less tactile experience: It would obviously be less tactile, since writing by hand provides that certain level of physical connection and sensory experience which online journaling often lacks.

Reliance on technology: Digital journaling requires one to own a device and power.

Digital journaling apps are making their application get much more expansive and far less easy—which you can only imagine—in all features. If you would feel better with a simple note-taking app or you would see yourself opening a web of multimedia interaction in one way or another, then digital support is for you.

MAINTAINING PRIVACY AND SECURITY IN DIGITAL JOURNALS

One of the most fundamental concerns with digital journaling is how to keep personal thoughts safe. It is very important to take proper precautions when journaling because of the very personal nature of journaling.

Here's some advice to help you keep an electronic journal private and secure:

Password strength: Set a strong password for your journal application. Avoid simple passwords that would easily give away information to others. You might consider using a password manager to keep your credentials safe.

Turn on encryption: If your journaling application happens to support encryption, turn it on. Encryption helps protect your entries from people with unauthorized access, even if they get their hands on your device.

Update your application frequently: Make sure not only your journaling application, but also your operating system and related software are updated regularly. Often, certain updates will help fix security vulnerabilities.

Back up entries: Make sure you back up your journal entries from time to time to a secure location, such as a highly secure cloud service. That way, if something happens to your device, you won't lose the entries.

Consider offline options: Many available journaling applications also have offline modes that allow you to write and save your entries even when you are not online. This way, your personal journal will not be compromised by online vulnerabilities.

Be careful about sharing: If you decide to share entries, consider your comfort level with public privacy. Think about whether sharing some of the information you have chosen to enter could put _you and/or others_ at risk.

Take all of this into account when considering your personal safety, as both the security and privacy of your digital journal are kept in mind. By taking these steps, you will be able to enjoy the full benefits of digital journaling without compromising your privacy.

Mixing Traditional and Digital: Hybrid Journaling

Hybrid journaling takes you to the best of both worlds, where traditional paper journaling meets today's modern digital tools. It allows you to retain the touch and feel of handwriting with the organization and multimedia capabilities of the digital medium.

Here are some exercises to practice hybrid journaling:

Scan or photograph your journal entries: Once you have written in your paper journal, scan or photograph your entries to preserve them digitally. This way, you can organize, search, and back up your entries while still having the original physical journal.

Paper journaling with digital prompts: You can look up prompts in journaling apps or websites and then write your answers back in your paper journal. Here we find a more tangible benefit to the inspiration and guidance from the digital sources: the traditional medium remains unchanged.

Digital supplements: Just as you can add photos, videos, or links to your journal, you can create a digital counterpart to your paper journal. For example, you can write in your paper journal and store related media or elaborations on a digital platform.

Sync across devices: This is typically for the hybrid journaler who prefers to write by hand but uses digital tools to organize all of their records. You may handwrite in a paper journal and then type in points or reflections in a digital application so that you have your insights with you at all times.

Track habits or goals digitally: When you track your habits or set your goals with your journal, you have a digital record of your progress and a notebook to write about your experiences.

Hybrid journaling offers a lot of flexibility. You can hybridize the practice in any way you like, using a combination of traditional and digital methods. You will find the best way that fits your life and empowers you to develop skills in reflection, creation, and growth.

5.2 CREATIVE JOURNALING METHODS

Journaling with Meditation: Writing as a Mindfulness Practice

Journaling can be a very powerful way to practice mindfulness and meditation. It is done together to increase the individual's level of self-awareness, thereby reducing stress from various sources and building a deep sense of being in everyday life.

Here is how to combine journaling with meditation:

Begin with a meditation session: Begin with a short meditation to calm your mind and focus your thoughts. This can be a simple breathing exercise, a guided meditation, or a mindfulness practice that helps you center yourself.

Write immediately after your meditation: Open your journal right after you finish meditating and begin writing. Try to capture any insights, feelings, or thoughts you may have had during meditation. Writing immediately after meditation can help maintain the clarity and calm experienced during meditation.

Use mindfulness prompts: Use mindfulness prompts, such as "What am I feeling at this moment?" or "What am I grateful for today?" to bring yourself back into the present, back into your body.

Reflect on your meditation practice: Record in your journal any moments of difficulty, progress, or insight that occur during or after meditation. Then reflect on the practice and its unfolding, and consider how these things might affect the rest of your life.

Work on mindful writing: Engage in daily writing with full awareness of the activity of writing. Paying attention to the movements of the pen, the texture of the paper, and the rhythm of your breath will help you stay grounded in the present moment.

Combining these two practices brings out the best in both journaling and meditation, helping you to view your inner world with the highest possible level of clarity and awareness. Very powerful in cultivating mindfulness and improving overall well-being.

USING PROMPTS FOR SELF-DISCOVERY: DEEPENING YOUR UNDERSTANDING OF SELF

Journaling prompts serve as stimulants to focus on questions or statements that incite you to reflect and explore yourself. These can really be quite helpful to allow you to get to know more about yourself and the thoughts or beliefs and desires you might have that are not readily visible.

Here are few prompts to start your self-discovery process:

Who am I really? Think about what you stand for-your core values, beliefs, and identity. What is distinctive about you? What are the fundamental character elements?

What are my greatest fears? Name them. Analyze what holds you back, even if it manifests itself subtly in your life, and what you can do to overcome it.

What are my greatest strengths? We all have something that makes us unique. Identify your strengths and how they contribute to your success and happiness. How can you use these strengths to achieve your goals?

What does success mean to me? Define what success has to do with you, beyond what everyone else thinks. How do you define a fulfilled and successful life?

What do I want my life to be? Think about the goals, relationships, and experiences you want to create. How can you make them a reality?

What does my ideal day look like? Picture a normal, perfect day. What are you doing that makes it so great? What are you doing, who are you with, and where are you right now? And how can you bring elements of that ideal day into your everyday life?

What legacy do I want to leave? Think about what kind of impact you want to have in the world or on those around you. What contributions you'd like to make and how you'd like to be remembered.

Self-Discovery Prompts can help you dig deeper into your thoughts and feelings to gain new insights and guidance for personal growth. It is a helpful tool that helps people understand themselves and align their lives with their true desires.

Time Capsule Journaling, Writing Letters to Your Future Self

The Time Capsule Journal appears as very personal letters or entries addressed to future readers. This allows you to capture any thought, goal, or even dream you may have while setting intentions for the future. Years from now, when you read them again, the effect is powerful, reminding you of your growth and the journey you have taken.

To create a time capsule journal

Choose a time frame: Think about when you'd like your time capsule entry to be found. Maybe a year from now, five years from now, or even a decade from now. Think about where you hope your life will be or what changes you may have experienced by then.

Think about your current life: What is your life like right now? What are you experiencing, how do you feel? What challenges or opportunities are you facing? Your daily life; your relationships; your work: Be as specific as possible. Be intentional: Use the opportunity of entering the time capsule to set intentions with your future self. What do you hope to have accomplished? What is important for you to live by as a value or set of habits? Write as if you were addressing these words of wisdom or inspiration to your future self.

Seal it: Once you've finished writing your time capsule entry, put it in a place where you won't be tempted to look at it until the time is right to refer to it. This could take the form of a real journal, a sealed envelope, or a digital document with a future reminder.

Time capsules revisited: When the time is right, open your time capsule entry and reflect on how life has changed since you wrote it. What goals have you been able to achieve? What are the things that seem most important now? Use this reflection as a guide.

Time-capsule journaling is a powerful way to connect with your future self and keep track of your personal growth. It's a way to embody how you might behave-with reflection, intention, and a touch of nostalgia. A really great way to see how you might have changed over time.

CONCLUSION

Advanced levels of journaling concepts take the practice to new heights by integrating technology, exploring creative methods, and building self-awareness. Whether you're blending digital tools with analog journaling, using prompts to know what's on your mind, or writing letters to your future self, these are unlocking possibilities for journaling and deeper personal growth. As you learn these advanced practices, remember that you are journaling in the deepest corner of your private life, and there is no right or wrong way to do it. The key is to find something that resonates with you, that allows you to express your thoughts, feelings, and ideas in a way that supports your growth and well-being.

SIX
TROUBLESHOOTING AND OVERCOMING OBSTACLES

6.1 MAINTAINING CONSISTENCY

K EEPING THE HABIT ALIVE: STRATEGIES

Doing a journal is very powerful, but because of the benefits it holds, one needs to keep at it with consistency to see its very many benefits. People can often start off with great enthusiasm, but usually get caught up with the pressures of life after a few days or weeks. So the way to make journaling stick: Consistency. Below are three strategies to help keep your new habit alive:

Specify the time: Settle on a specific time during the day for journaling. It could be every morning, during lunchtime, or even just before going to bed. Having a specified time helps in enculturating the practice within your daily routine. Strong consistency in timing enforces the habit and allows it to be conducted with ease.

Start small: Don't task yourself with unrealistic expectations. Maybe a few minutes per day or just a single sentence or paragraph could be a target. The main idea is to start since after that, the writing process might become easier.

Use prompts: On days you feel like you can't find anything to write about, use prompts to get your mind active and jogging. Prompts may give you a point of reference or an inspiration, simply to get over the blank edit and retain the habit of journaling.

ATTACH JOURNALING TO ANOTHER HABIT

Tie journaling to something you are already doing, such as your morning coffee or brushing of teeth at bedtime. This is referred to as habit stacking. It may help you reinforce the new habit by attaching it to something you do regularly already.

Keep your journal accessible: Keep your journal in a place you regularly see, like your nightstand, desk or the kitchen counter. Leaving your journal out in the open helps encourage you to write in it.

Reward yourself: Celebrate your consistency through rewards when you reach the major points or come back to journaling regularly for a week or month. Let the rewards be small, such as watching one of your favorite movies, as a showcase of self-love.

Be flexible: Well, sometimes life may be surprising, and there might be days when journaling isn't wide open. Instead, give yourself permission to skip one day rather than brooding over it. The important thing is not to be too hard on yourself and let it get in the way of your progress.

This way, you can put in place strategies that don't just help you institute a journaling practice but make it a consistent and even natural, rewarding part of your daily going-ons.

DEALING WITH LIFE'S DISRUPTIONS: HOW TO GET BACK ON TRACK

Even the most devoted journalers are thrown off by massive life changes, huge schedules, or a motivation drop that can make it actually quite hard to keep the consistency going. Fortunately, you can always get back into the groove, no matter how long ago it was since you last kept a journal.

Here is how to relaunch your journaling practice after it's been disrupted:

Recognize the disruption: Life is what happens to all of us, and you should know that any process of building a habit has its own ups and downs. It's normal to experience setbacks; rather than feeling guilt or disappointment, you might want to remind yourself that this is part of it.

Start Over: A lot of times, resuming journaling is simply a matter of starting over in your mind. You might wish to start a new journal or perhaps, eventually, a new section in the journal in which you write. This new start will be symbolic in that it helps you break through any of those negative feelings that such interruption creates.

Reflect on the disturbance: Use your journal to reflect on what caused the disruption and how you felt as a result of the issue. Sometimes, being able to articulate challenges that have been presented to you can help you work through your feelings and find ways to avoid those kinds of setbacks in the future.

Set a new goal: Set a new unrealistic goal-that is, a very small achievable goal to get back in. Example: make a goal to just be committed to journaling for five minutes each day this week. Reaching this can start to rebuild your momentum and confidence.

Give yourself a prompt: If you find it hard to start, give yourself a simple prompt to help you ease your way back into journaling. For instance, "What has changed since I last journaled?" or "What do I want to focus on this week?

Be kind to yourself: The process of getting back on track should be approached with self-compassion. Without self-criticism, you put more positivity into the fact that this is one sure step — you are returning to the journal.

Recall your motivation: Think back to the reason you started journaling in the first place. Being able to reconnect with your original motivation can once again ignite the love you need for the practice and keep you committed.

With this mindset and the set of steps for restarting towards that disruption, one will be in a very successful position to re-establish the journaling habit and continue his growth out of this powerful practice.

KNOWING WHEN TO TAKE A BREAK

Having insisted on consistency, one should also know when to take a break from journaling. As with any habits that have been formed, there will be times when journaling may feel like an added rather than welcome burden. Should one experience the times of day that they have set aside for journaling with broad trepidation, or should one feel overwhelmed by the expectations that lay in waiting for them during those moments, then perhaps the time has come to step back.

Here is how to know if it is time to take a break from journaling:

When it is leading to burnout: If journaling has started to feel exhausting and you are experiencing burnout, then maybe this is a time to take a break. Forcing oneself through burnout will have the negative consequences of associating this activity with everything bad, which could make it just that much harder when one desires to go back into it with a positive mindset.

Lack of Enjoyment: Writing should be a fulfilling and enjoyable activity, and if an individual has begun to feel that journaling is no longer a pleasure, then probably this is the time to take a step back and reconsider the approach. You can take a break in order to fall back in love with journaling.

Overwhelm or stress: Sometimes life can be overwhelming, and carving out time to journal while everything is already on the plate can really push the stress over the edge. If this is just one more thing to do on an overwhelming list, and you feel that it might be best to take a brief pause, do so.

Finding words could be difficult: If you constantly feel as though you're grappling for the words or grappling for topics to write about, this could be a big indicator that you need to take a break. You might just need a bit of time away before coming back to your writing with new ideas and inspiration.

Physical or emotional fatigue: Writing needs a great amount of physical and mental agility. If you are physically or emotionally fatigued, you would be better off resting than forcing some writing out.

Taking a break doesn't make you a failure as a journaler; sometimes, getting back to an activity needs time, and it's good when this pause happens at an appropriate time. When you do decide to resume journaling, approach it with a fresh perspective and a sense of excitement.

6.2 MANAGING SELF-CRITICISM

Shushing the Inner Critic: Writing Without Judgment

Self-criticism is one of the greatest challenges for being able to journal properly. The inner critic—that voice inside your head doubting your worth, abilities, and each and every word—makes daring, or perhaps even writing in a journal, seem like an impossible thing to do. You can write freely and authentically only if you teach yourself how to shut it down.

Here's how you can work to get past self-criticism in journaling:

Recognize the inner critic: The first step to changing self-criticism is being able to first recognize that it exists. Is this voice part of you, but not you? Having identified it, the voice can then be separated from self.

Practice self-compassion: Start treating yourself as kindly as you would your best friend. Counteract self-criticism by using self-compassionate responses. If you are thinking, "This writing isn't good enough," reply, "It is okay to write imperfectly. This is my space to explore and grow."

Write for yourself: Your journal is for your eyes alone, and you are not there to impress anybody, not even yourself. Let go of perfection and focus on writing for your benefit. A journal allows you to express your thoughts and feelings-no judgments.

Embrace imperfection: Let yourself cringe just a little at writing that is less than perfect. Allow for mistakes, messy handwriting, and incomplete thoughts; they all come with this process. Allow the imperfections to be quintessentially a part of journaling, and let yourself write without fear of mistakes.

Employ free writing: Free writing is a practice wherein you continuously write for certain amounts of time without allowing yourself to stop and edit. This practice may quiet the inner critic by encouraging one to attend to the flow of writing rather than the quality of the content.

Challenge bad thoughts: When thoughts go to a self-critical place, question the validity of thoughts. Even think: "Is this thought true? What evidence do I have in support of this thought? What advantages or disadvantages would there be to a friend who had this thought?"

Allow yourself to create a safe space: make your environment in journaling as safe as possible and comforting. Surround yourself with things that inspire and relax you; remind yourself this is your private time to explore your thoughts without the fear of judgment.

You will learn how to quiet the inner critic and develop a more authentic, releasing, and enjoyable journaling practice. In time, such practice can nurture the facets of self-confidence and develop a lot more positive relationship with yourself.

EMBRACING IMPERFECTION: ALLOW YOUR JOURNAL TO BE A SAFE SPACE

Your journal is the one place where you allow yourself to be imperfect, without the compulsion to be perfect. Poor journaling means accepting imperfection with free rein to explore your thoughts, emotions, and experiences honestly without fear. It's important to create a space in which one can express themselves fully, knowing they are not being judged by themselves or others.

Here's how you can bring imperfection into your whole journaling journey:

Drop expectations: On the note of letting go of any expectations around what your journal should be or look like, or your journal entries. Your journal does NOT have to look perfect or presentable or organized. If it does that then great, but just remember it's usually a mess inside your head.

Process > Product : Journaling is about the writing, not what you write. Change your mentality from crafting a "perfect" journal to enjoying the process of putting word on paper. Permit yourself to write whatever sans being concerned about the outcome.

Write without editing: Allow yourself to write without stopping to edit or revise. Let your mind flow and, in that process, fragmented or unclear thoughts are also okay. You can revise or improve what has been written later on should you choose to, but the initial state of writing should be about expression and not perfection.

Allow mistakes: By nature, journaling is prone to mistakes. Sometimes you'll spell a word wrong, or cross one out, or write something that just doesn't make complete sense. Allow these "flaws" into your journal. Mistakes are part of the authenticity of your journal.

Experiment and play: The journal is not just a journal, but rather a place for trying new writing styles, formats, or ideas. Don't shy away from something just because it's risky or what would be considered unconventional. Journaling should be that open place to explore creativity.

Go with the flow: There will be days of inspired writing, full of insight, and days where your words sound flat or contrived. Permit this to be part of the more natural up-and-down activity associated with maintaining a journal. As with getting lost on a hike, there are rarely wrong turns in the journal, and each entry, imperfect as it may be, furthers your overall growth.

It just allows for a sense of freedom and self-acceptance by embracing all the imperfections that come with your journaling practice. It's a situation that encourages one to freely express their thoughts and emotions without feeling obliged to any standard, making the journal a true safe space to self-express.

USING JOURNALING AS A TOOL FOR SELF-COMPASSION

Self-compassion is being kind, understanding, and supportive to oneself when in trouble or failing. Journaling could be a powerful tool to install self-compassion in mind—communicating even more loving and accepting a relationship with oneself.

Here's how to use journaling for self-compassion:

Write to yourself as you would to your friend: When it arises in any challenging situation, or giving in to a near incapacitating feeling of self-doubt, then write back to affirmative thinking with encouragement, understanding, and supporting dialogue you would express toward someone you do care about.

Acknowledge what you feel: Write in your journal to acknowledge and validate your feelings, but free of judgment. Write about what you feel and why, to allow yourself to feel and think about your feelings.

Self-forgiveness practice: Every time one feels guilty, shameful, or regretful, he must practice self-forgiveness through his journal. He jots down what happened, how it felt at the time, and why you should forgive yourself. Remind yourself that people do make mistakes.

Cultivate gratitude about yourself: Write about your traits you like in yourself and the good things you have done. Ingraining self-gratitude helps get that focus away from those things you may view as imperfections and move it toward what makes you distinctly special and worth something.

Set intentions for self-care: Use the journal to set some well-being intentions physically and emotionally. One full page—about being kinder to yourself, things you can do for self-care, and ways to focus on your well-being.

Reflect on strengths: Think back on your strengths and qualities that helped you lead through adversities courtesy of the past. Write down how the strengths continue to support you in your life and how leaning on them in tough times brings you solace.

Practice loving-kindness: Engage in a loving-kindness meditation through journaling. Write about sending love, compassion, and kindness to yourself, and to others. This practice helps develop a sense of connection and compassion, within yourself and with others.

Journaling for self-compassion aids in the development of a much kinder and more understanding relationship with oneself. Through continuous practice of self-compassion in the journal, build resilience, lessen self-criticism, and help cultivate the sense of inner peace within.

CONCLUSION

Overcoming the obstacles in your practice is a natural process. If the difficulties are either sustaining regularity, working against self-critique, or learning how to truly embrace imperfection, each is hard and thereby offers profound occasions for growth and self-discovery. You then apply strategies from this chapter to more easily navigate the challenges and make real journaling practice deep and strong. Remember, journaling is a very personal and dynamic process. It is not about perfection or meeting certain standards but about exploring your thoughts, emotions, and experiences in ways that support your growth and well-being. Stay connected to your practice, especially when it gets difficult; the rewards from journaling will come in waves, being a potent form of expression, healing, and transformation.

SEVEN
THE TRANSFORMATIONAL POWER OF JOURNALING

7.1 JOURNALING FOR PERSONAL DEVELOPMENT

REFLECTING ON YOUR JOURNEY: HOW JOURNALING SUPPORTS PERSONAL DEVELOPMENT

Well, journaling is not just a record of events but a potent tool for growth. In this regard, it reflects on the thinking, feeling, and experience of an individual to allow him or her to gain increased insight into himself or herself and his or her journey in life. It allows one to trace progress, identify patterns, and realize changes in beliefs, attitude, and behavior over time.

So journaling aids personal development in the following ways:

Increased self-awareness: The act of journaling itself makes you self-aware of your own thoughts, emotions, and reactions. Once you become regular with writing about experiences, you begin to find patterns in behavioral change and thinking. This sharpens your self-awareness and increases the capacity to make more deliberate choices, allowing you to keep actions in line with values and goals.

Goal Setting and Achievement: Jotting down your goals in a journal makes you clear your intention and subsequently set them as achievable steps. If you return to them, updating the plan, it's always helpful. The facility with obtaining review and alternation of goals at different points of life keeps you on the path of checking progress, and hence, you are motivated. Also, remember what journaling is capable of: reflection. How do you overcome hindrances and be on the path of all-round growth?.

Emotional processing: Journaling offers a secure outlet to process and work through hard emotions like anger, sadness, or anxiety. By writing out your feelings, you can discover the underlying causes and find healthy ways to deal with them. This processing makes you quite resilient emotionally, with more stability.

Learning from experiences: Your reflection from the journal about all that transpired in the past results in an enriched insight about valuable lessons that may subsequently guide future actions. You will be able to make better decisions and not repeat the same mistake again by understanding what worked and what didn't.

Cultivating gratitude and positivity: The act of gratitude journaling somehow makes you appreciate the positive attributes in your life. Writing on a regular basis about the things you are grateful for will enable you to cultivate your mind toward positivity, hence bringing an improvement to your general well-being and happiness.

Building Self-Confidence: Through journaling, the growth of your self-confidence is very high, as you document all the accomplishments, strengths, and development that you have undergone. Journaling will make you celebrate even the seemingly minor successes and take note of accomplishments realized over a period.

Tracking personal growth: Another strong suit of journaling is the capacity to have a look back at your entries and see how much you've grown. Rereading entries from past periods in your life, you can track how your evolution has gone along other paths—relationships, career, personal development.

When used regularly, journaling can bring about a transformative power for changing things around that facilitates personal development and growth. It serves much more to act as a tool for self-reflection, goal-setting, and emotional processing in ways that help live a more fulfilling and meaningful life.

JOURNAL KEEPING AND EMOTIONAL INTELLIGENCE: KNOWING AND MANAGING YOUR EMOTIONS

EI means ability of a person to realize and understand his or her feelings along with the feelings of the others and to manage his emotions along with the emotions of the others. Among the most practicable processes of developing and enhancing emotional intelligence is journaling, which gives one an avenue to explore and process his or her emotions in a more structured and reflective approach.

This is how journaling would assist you in improving your emotional intelligence:

Identification of emotions: Journaling helps one identify an awfully large amount of one's personal emotions. Writing routinely about the way you feel enhances your emotional vocabulary and your knowledge in regard to the states of your emotions. That is the first step to being more emotionally intelligent.

Identification of triggers: The events, thoughts, or behaviors that tend to bring about some emotions will be clear through journaling. Being aware of exactly what your triggers are means you can control and anticipate emotional outbreaks.

Emotion Processing: When you pen down your feelings, you give yourself a safe space for processing and eventually working your way through them. This is different from suppression or avoidance; journaling allows and even urges one to confront and make sense of his or her feelings, leading to much emotional clarity and stability.

Developing empathy: Journaling about your interactions with others can enhance your ability to empathize. By reflecting on how others might feel or why they acted in a certain way, you can develop a more compassionate and empathetic perspective.

Regulation of emotion: This is a component of emotional intelligence. Keeping a journal helps with the practice of emotional regulation for pausing, reflecting, and responding, as opposed to reacting impulsively. This likely leads to more control over emotions with time and building resilience.

Emotional intelligence/self-awareness: There is a really close association between emotional intelligence and self-awareness. Through the frequent practice of journaling, one becomes much more familiar with one's trend of emotions, points of strength, and patterns of weakness that one needs to work on. This self-awareness forms a very important link in decision-making and maintaining emotional balance.

Better communication: By becoming more emotionally intelligent through your journaling, you will experience a significantly positive change in your communication. Clarity, assertiveness, and a sure sense of empathy in your communication can all arise out of an understanding of your own and other people's feelings and moods.

Journaling fosters emotional intelligence, so that it would be through forming relationships, making decisions, and growing healthily that the well-being would increase. That's to enhance the quality of relationships and increment in decision-making.

BUILDING RESILIENCE: HOW JOURNALING HELPS IN OVERCOMING CHALLENGES

Resilience is the ability to bounce back after adversity and cope with life's challenges. Journaling can be so potent for resilience building and enhancing because this is a space that any person can apply to reflect on issues, difficulties, solutions, and retain a positive outlook.

Here is how journaling can help build resilience:

Adversity processing: By helping you to process your thoughts and feelings when going through challenges, journal writing offers a healthy means to overcome them. Writing about your experiences helps you make sense of the difficult situations and lowers the emotional burden, hence enabling you to move on easily.

Perspective: Journaling will urge you to step back and look at your challenges from a broader perspective; reflecting on the difficulties of the past that you have surmounted can remind you of your strength and resilience, boosting your confidence in facing current challenges.

Problem-solving: Writing about your challenges opens you to the potential solutions and ways out. Journaling really gives room for brainstorming, weighing pros and cons, and planning your steps, hence being proactive in facing adversity.

Reframing Negative Thoughts: Very frequently, resilience involves changing a frame of thought from a negative one to a positive one. Journaling will help to frame your negative thoughts in a different light by ensuring that you focus on what you can control, what you have learned from the situation, and how you can grow from the challenge.

Practicing gratitude: To develop resilience, try keeping a journal of all the things in your life that you are grateful for—whether or not you tend to dwell on those thoughts when you feel low. Gratitude shifts your focus from what's going wrong in your life to what's going right and fosters an optimistic and resilient attitude.

Tracking progress: Putting down into a journal the challenges you have faced and how you overcame them will allow you to reflect on just how far you have come. Being able to look back on how far you have come can enable your resilience by showing you that you are capable of overcoming any challenges.

Sustaining Hope: Journaling can help one speak about their hopes and desires, no matter how discouraging everything may seem. Through their reflection on goals and desired futures, a sense of direction may be reaffirmed, which is a key ingredient in resilience.

Journaling to build resilience will help you face the highs and lows of life with increased ease and confidence. Jotting down reflections on a regular basis will really help you strengthen your ability to positively overcome adversity, keep expecting good things in life, and continue growing stronger because of the trials and tribulations you encounter.

7.2 THE LEGACY OF YOUR JOURNAL

JOURNALLING FOR FUTURE GENERATIONS: LEAVE A WRITTEN LEGACY

Your journal is more than just a record of your feelings and experiences; it can be your legacy for others to benefit from for generations to come. With a journal, you can transform your vast personal history, values, and wisdom into a transferable form through which future generations can experience and learn from who you are. Much of the target audience would be family members and friends, and of course readers in general. A journal will be the document that preserves one's life.

Here are a couple of ways to approach journaling with future generations in mind:

Documenting your life story: In your journal, record the milestones, events in your life, childhood, family history, career, relationships, and experiences that seem important. These entries form a narrative that others can learn from and identify with in the future.

Values and Beliefs: Reflect on the values, beliefs, and guiding principles in your life. You might write about what is really important to you and why. By sharing your values in your journal, you leave an opportunity for future generations to understand your worldview and, hopefully, the legacy you will leave behind.

Advice and wisdom: Your journal could one day be considered advice or even wise words for another person. You can write about lessons learned, adversities, and insights you've gotten with time. Addressing entries to specific people, such as your children or your grandchildren, offering guidance based on what you believe they could learn from in your journey.

Preserve family traditions and memories: Use your journal to document family traditions, stories, and memories. Write about holidays, special occasions, and the people who have shaped your life. These entries help preserve the culture and heritage of your family for future generations.

Reflect on current events: Journal your thoughts and feelings concerning the major events of your time: political developments, social movements, or technological advances. Your reflection provides perspective from a personal standpoint about the historical events through which you have lived.

Think about privacy and sharing: Suppose you are planning to share your journal with the future generations, in that case, you must reflect on what are the parts you do not mind being private and the parts that you are okay to share. You might want to make separate journals that detail varying types of content or explicitly state your wish for different handling of private and public journal parts after your death.

Consider format and preservation: Think about how you will preserve your journal for future generations. Physical journals can be passed down, but they are also susceptible to damage. You may want to consider digitizing your entries to ensure they are preserved long-term. If you keep a digital journal, make sure it's backed up and accessible.

Your journal becomes a legacy that imparts an insight, wisdom, and connection to future generations. The documenting of life, the recording of one's values—a written record, presumably, to inspire or perhaps even to guide others after you're gone.

TURNING JOURNALS INTO MEMOIRS: WRITING YOUR LIFE STORY

For some, a journal will be a stepping stone to a memoir. Your journal may be the starting point towards writing this story in a more formalized and polished way, describing your experiences from beginning until the end. Whether ready for publication or not, turning your journal into a memoir allows you to deeply reflect on your experiences and share that journey with others.

Here's how to use your journal to write a memoir:

Review your journal entries: Take a close look at the entries in your journals to decide on the key themes, events, and periods in your life that stand out. Look for patterns, turning points, and moments of growth that can form the backbone of your memoir.

Create an outline: From your review, go ahead to arrange how you will present your memoir. Plan out your life-story in chapters or sections focusing on major periods or experiences. It is fine if your outline is not rigid — let it grow and adapt as you write.

Elaborate on key moments: Use your journal entries as a springboard, but give greater detail to key moments, filling in background and expanding on reflection. Think about the ways these experiences have shaped who you are and what you've learned from them.

Set a central theme: Most memoirs are based on a theme; such may include, an experience, overcoming a situation one was in, following a dream, or the relationships between people. Get a central theme of your life and develop it through the body of your memoir.

Second, **add narrative elements to your writing**: memoirs often include dialogue, descriptions, and setting scenes. While you're writing, think about how you can add versatility to your story: you can rely on your journal entries to remember details, but feel free to embellish, or even invent, as long as it serves your story best.

Reflect on your journey: A memoir isn't just a re-telling of the facts, it's a reflection on your journey and what it means to you. Use your memoir for a deeper look into the experiences—their very meaning, how they shaped you, and in what ways you grew.

Edit and Revise: Before or after writing your memoir, set it aside or you may keep it and edit it later on. Editing will help improve your story, clear your message, and ensure that your memoir resonates with whoever reads it. You may seek other opinions from close friends who can be trusted or share with peers in your writing group.

Consider your audience: A memoir is all about you, your life, and experiences, but you must keep in mind who your target readers are. Writing for your family, a general readership, or just for yourself makes a difference in how you write and in terms of having your memoir actually touch other readers significantly.

Turning your journal into a memoir is one of the most rewarding things one can do. It allows the writer to narrate their story in a way that feels meaningful, recapture their journey, share the experience, and bequeath to the world some things they value.

ETHICAL CONCERNS OF JOURNALING: PRIVACY, HONESTY, AND INTEGRITY

And because journaling is a truly personal thing, it does have considerations to be ethical, especially if you are going to share or publish your journal. Above all, an individual needs to deal with journaling with the highest sense of responsibility there is, with regard to issues such as privacy, accuracy, and honesty.

Here are some of the ethical considerations:

Respect other peoples' privacy: When writing about others in your journal, especially when you plan to have the entries published or shared, their privacy needs to be respected. Avoid identifiable data, as well as sensitive information that might make someone suffer with it. If you are going to write about other individuals, protect their identity with pseudonyms or changes in details.

Honesty and Authenticity: The best way to journal is to be honest and authentic. Write about your feelings, thoughts, and experiences confidently, even if uncomfortable. Of course, being honest does not mean you need to share everything; just be mindful with what you are willing or not willing to tell, especially when sharing with others.

Integrity in personal reflection: Journaling is a personal, mental tool of self-reflection intended for growth. You are to experience your writing with integrity—a way of being open to your self-examination of your actions, beliefs, and biases. Do not use this journal as a way to manage or place blame somewhere else. This journal should be used to achieve self-awareness and personal accountability.

Mindful sharing: If you choose to share your diary or parts of it, do so mindfully. Consider the impact your words might have on others and the potential consequences of making your private thoughts public. Sharing your journal might make you feel empowered, but at the same time, it should be done responsibly, considering how this might be taken. –

Consent and collaboration: If your diary includes stories or information about others, especially close to you, consider taking their consent to share or publish the journal. When collaboration is in sight, involve them in the process to represent their perspective in the best possible manner.

Balancing truth and fiction: For a memoir, if you change it from a journal, you will mostly have to balance between basing your work on truth and storytelling. While essentially it's brought out in its reality, factor how the creative liberties taken at this point will still hold up the element of truth in your story.

Ethical journaling is having a consideration or sensitivity about possible impacts your words may evoke in you and others. Through honest, respectful, and integral writing, one can achieve a fulfilling and responsible journal-writing practice.

EIGHT
JOURNALING AND TECHNOLOGY: BALANCING DIGITAL TOOLS WITH ANALOG PRACTICES

In an age where our lives are intertwined with technology, journaling is at a crossroads. The lure of digital convenience beckons, while the tactile satisfaction of pen and paper endures. This chapter explores the landscape of digital journaling and guides you through the intricate dance between pixels and paper.

DIGITAL JOURNALING: A NEW FRONTIER

Digital journaling apps have revolutionized the way we record our thoughts. These virtual notebooks offer features unimaginable in their paper counterparts. Imagine searching through years of entries in seconds, or adding photos and voice memos to your daily reflections. The possibilities go as far as our digital imaginations allow.

Popular apps like Day One, Journey, and Penzu lead the way, each offering unique features. Day One excels at multimedia integration, allowing you to weave photos, audio, and even location data into your entries. Journey emphasizes cross-platform accessibility, ensuring that your journal travels with you across devices. Penzu prioritizes security, offering military-grade encryption for your most private thoughts.

THE DIGITAL DILEMMA: PROS AND CONS

Digital journaling has many advantages. Unlimited storage means you never run out of pages. Cloud synchronization keeps your entries safe from physical damage or loss. The ability to edit and reorganize entries offers flexibility that analog journals can't match.

But the digital realm isn't without its drawbacks. Screen fatigue can discourage long writing sessions. The ever-present distractions of notifications and apps threaten to derail your focus. And for some, the intangible nature of digital text lacks the emotional connection of handwritten words.

CHOOSING YOUR DIGITAL TOOLS

Choosing the right digital journaling tool requires introspection. Consider your priorities. Do you value seamless multimedia integration? Prioritize apps with robust photo and audio capabilities. Is privacy your primary concern? Look for end-to-end encryption and local storage options. Are you journaling on multiple devices? Look for apps with reliable cross-platform synchronization.

Experiment with different apps. Many offer free trials so you can test their interfaces and features. Pay attention to how each app feels to use. The most feature-rich option may not be the one that inspires you to write consistently.

PROTECT YOUR DIGITAL THOUGHTS

Privacy concerns often deter potential digital journalists. But with the right precautions, your digital entries can be safer than a locked journal. Enable two-factor authentication in your journaling application.

Use a unique, strong password. If your app offers encryption, turn it on.

Be aware of cloud storage. While convenient, it introduces additional security considerations. Research your chosen app's data handling practices. Some offer "zero-knowledge" encryption, meaning that even the company can't access your entries.

For highly sensitive content, consider keeping those entries locally on your device rather than in the cloud. Some apps offer this as an option for specific entries or notebooks.

BEYOND TEXT: MULTIMEDIA JOURNALING

Digital journals break free from the limitations of text-only entries. Embrace the multimedia potential. Take a photo of a beautiful sunset and write about the emotions it evokes. Record an audio clip of a street musician and describe how the melody moved you. Add sketches, diagrams, or mind maps to visualize your thoughts.

Experiment with different media to express yourself. A voice memo might capture the raw emotion of a moment better than written words. A collage of images might illustrate a complex feeling better than paragraphs of text.

THE HYBRID APPROACH: BRIDGING DIGITAL AND ANALOG

For many, the ideal journaling practice combines digital and analog methods. This hybrid approach allows you to take advantage of the best of both worlds. Use a paper journal for deep, reflective writing sessions free from digital distractions. Turn to your digital journal for quick snapshots throughout the day, or for entries enriched with photos and audio.

To implement a hybrid system, establish clear roles for each medium. Your paper journal might be reserved for morning pages or evening reflections. Your digital journal could serve as a tool for capturing ideas on the go or as a multimedia diary of daily life.

Consider digitizing key entries from your paper journal. Scanning or photographing important pages creates a searchable backup and allows you to carry your most important reflections with you digitally.

OVERCOMING DIGITAL HURDLES

Digital journaling has unique challenges. Screen fatigue can make long writing sessions uncomfortable. Combat this by adjusting your device's display settings. Lower the brightness, use night mode, or try e-ink devices designed for extended reading and writing.

Distractions are another major hurdle. Notifications and the temptation to multitask can derail your journaling session. Create a distraction-free environment by using your device's Do Not Disturb mode. Some journaling apps offer focused writing modes that block out other apps and notifications.

For those who find typing less engaging than handwriting, explore apps that support stylus input. Writing on a tablet with a high-quality stylus can replicate much of the tactile experience of pen and paper.

THE FUTURE OF JOURNALING TECHNOLOGY

As technology evolves, so will digital journaling. Artificial intelligence could offer personalized writing prompts based on your previous entries. Virtual reality could create immersive journaling environments that transport you to a quiet beach or a cozy cabin for your writing sessions.

Voice-to-text technology continues to improve, potentially allowing you to seamlessly dictate your thoughts. Augmented reality may allow you to "place" digital journal entries in physical locations, creating a geographic memoir of your life.

While these advances offer exciting possibilities, remember the core purpose of journaling: self-reflection and personal growth. Embrace new technologies that enhance that purpose, but don't let the tools overshadow the practice.

FINDING YOUR DIGITAL-ANALOG BALANCE

Finding your ideal balance between digital and analog journaling requires experimentation. Try this exercise to discover your preferences:

1. Journal exclusively on paper for one week.
2. The following week, switch to a digital-only practice.
3. For the third week, combine both methods as you see fit.

After each week, reflect on your experience. Which method felt more natural? Where did you experience friction? Which approach led to deeper insights or more consistent writing?

Consider these questions:

- **When did you find yourself reaching for your journal the most?**
- **How did the different methods affect the content of your writing?**
- **Did you notice any changes in your emotional connection to the journaling process?**

Use these insights to create a personalized journaling practice that leverages the strengths of both digital and analog methods.

EMBRACING THE DIGITAL JOURNALING JOURNEY

As you navigate the world of digital journaling, remember that the tool serves the practice, not the other way around. Whether you're scribbling in a leather-bound notebook or tapping on a glass screen, the power of journaling lies in the act of reflection and self-expression.

Digital tools offer unprecedented flexibility and features, but they don't inherently make your journaling practice better or worse. The value comes from your commitment to show up, day after day, to have a conversation with yourself.

Approach digital journaling with curiosity and openness. Explore new features and apps, but don't let the search for the perfect tool distract you from the practice itself. Find what works for you, what inspires you to write consistently, and what helps you gain the most insight from your reflections.

In the end, the most powerful journaling app is the one that fades into the background, allowing your thoughts and feelings to flow freely onto the page-or screen. Whether you embrace the digital revolution, cling to pen and paper, or find a balance between the two, your journal remains a powerful tool for self-discovery and personal growth.

The future of journaling is not about choosing between digital and analog, but about creating a practice that seamlessly integrates both, enhancing your ability to record, reflect, and learn from your life's journey. As you continue to explore and refine your journaling practice, let technology be a tool that amplifies your voice, rather than drowning it in a sea of features and notifications.

Your journal, in whatever form it takes, is a testament to your experiences, your growth, and your inner world. Embrace the tools that resonate with you and let your unique voice shine through, one entry at a time.

NINE

JOURNALING FOR MENTAL HEALTH: MANAGING ANXIETY, DEPRESSION, AND STRESS

In the labyrinth of our minds, journaling serves as both map and compass. It illuminates the dark corners of our psyche and guides us toward understanding and healing. This chapter explores the profound impact journaling can have on mental health and offers specific techniques for navigating the turbulent waters of anxiety, depression, and stress.

THE THERAPEUTIC POWER OF THE PEN

Journaling goes beyond mere record-keeping; it becomes a dialogue with our deepest selves. Research consistently demonstrates its effectiveness in addressing mental health challenges. The act of writing externalizes our internal struggles, allowing us to observe our thoughts and emotions with greater objectivity.

Dr. James Pennebaker, a pioneer in writing therapy research, discovered that expressive writing can lead to improved mood, reduced anxiety, and better sleep quality. His studies show that writing about emotional experiences for as little as 15 minutes a day can significantly improve both physical and mental health.

CREATING YOUR MENTAL HEALTH JOURNALING PRACTICE

To tap into the therapeutic potential of journaling, create a dedicated space and time for the practice. Choose a quiet, comfortable place where you can write without interruption. Set aside at least 15-20 minutes each day, preferably at the same time each day, to establish a routine.

Your journal will become a safe haven. It is a place where you can express yourself without fear of judgment or repercussions. Write freely and let your thoughts and feelings flow onto the page without censorship. Remember, this journal is for your eyes only - honesty with yourself is paramount.

ANXIETY JOURNALING: TAMING THE WHIRLWIND OF WORRY

Anxiety often manifests as a tornado of what-ifs and worst-case scenarios. Journaling can help ground you in reality and give you perspective. Try these techniques:

1. **Worry journals**: Document your anxious thoughts in detail. What are you worried about? How likely is this scenario to occur? What evidence supports or refutes this worry?
2. **Cognitive Restructuring**: Challenge anxious thoughts through writing. Identify cognitive distortions such as catastrophizing or all-or-nothing thinking. Reframe these thoughts in a more balanced, realistic way.
3. **Exposure Journaling**: For specific phobias or fears, write about exposing yourself to the feared situation. Describe the scenario in vivid detail, including your physical sensations and emotional reactions. Regular exposure through writing can desensitize you to the fear over time.

Example:

"My heart races at the thought of public speaking. My palms sweat and my mouth goes dry. But I've spoken in public before and survived. People listened attentively. I didn't faint or forget everything. This presentation won't be perfect, but it doesn't have to be. I'm prepared, I know my material, and I'm going to do my best."

DEPRESSION JOURNALING: LIGHTING THE DARKNESS

Depression can cast a heavy shadow over our lives, distorting our perceptions and draining our energy. Journaling offers a lifeline, a way to reconnect with ourselves and find glimmers of light in the darkness.

1. Gratitude Journaling: Each day, write down three things you're grateful for, no matter how small. This practice shifts the focus from what's missing to what's present and positive in your life.
2. Positive Experience Recording: Describe in detail a positive experience you had today. What happened? How did it make you feel? This helps combat the negative bias often present in depression.
3. Track your accomplishments: Document your accomplishments, no matter how small they may seem. Brushing your teeth, making your bed, or sending an email all count. This counteracts feelings of worthlessness and highlights your abilities.

Example:

"Today I got out of bed. The weight of exhaustion pressed down, but I pushed through. I made coffee, the aroma of which filled the kitchen. The warmth of the mug in my hands anchored me in the present. I answered a work email. Small steps, but steps nonetheless. I'm still here, still trying."

MANAGING STRESS THROUGH WRITING

In our fast-paced world, stress has become a constant companion. Journaling provides a pressure release valve that allows us to process and manage stress more effectively.

1. **Keep a Stress Log**: Identify your stressors. What situations, people, or events cause stress? How does your body react? This awareness is the first step in developing coping strategies.
2. **Solution-focused journaling**: For each stressor, brainstorm possible solutions. What actions can you take to address the situation? What resources or support will you need?
3. Emotional Release Writing: Set a timer for 10 minutes and write non-stop about what's bothering you. Don't censor yourself - let it all out. When the time is up, destroy the paper if you wish. This cathartic release often provides immediate relief.

Example:

"Work deadlines are looming. Pressure building in my chest. Breathe. What can I control? I'll break the project into smaller tasks. I'll talk to my manager about prioritizing. I can't do everything at once, but I can do something. One step at a time."

MINDFULNESS AND SELF-COMPASSION EXERCISES

Incorporating mindfulness and self-compassion into your journaling practice enhances its therapeutic benefits. These exercises foster a kinder, more accepting relationship with yourself.

1. **Mindful observation**: Describe your current environment in detail, using all five senses. This grounds you in the present moment and interrupts cycles of rumination.

2. **Self-Compassion Letter**: Write a letter to yourself from the perspective of a loving, compassionate friend. What would they say about your current struggles? How would they offer encouragement and support?

3. **Body Scan Journaling**: Starting from your toes and moving up to your head, write about the sensations in each part of your body. This practice increases body awareness and can help you identify where you're holding stress or emotions.

TRACKING MOOD AND IDENTIFYING TRIGGERS

Regularly tracking your mood in your journal can reveal patterns and triggers that you might otherwise miss. Create a simple mood scale (1-10) and record your mood at consistent times throughout the day. Along the way, note significant events, interactions, or thoughts.

Over time, you'll begin to see connections. Perhaps your mood dips after certain social interactions or improves after exercise. With this knowledge, you can make informed decisions about your activities and environment.

SHARE YOUR JOURNAL: WHEN AND HOW

While your journal is primarily a private tool, sharing selected entries with a therapist can enhance your treatment. If you're working with a mental health professional, discuss how journaling can complement your therapy.

Your therapist can provide guidance on specific journaling techniques tailored to your needs. They may also offer insight into patterns or themes that emerge in your writing that you hadn't noticed.

You're in control when it comes to sharing. Choose entries that you're comfortable discussing. Remember, the goal is to support your therapeutic journey, not to reveal every private thought.

INTEGRATING JOURNALING WITH OTHER MENTAL HEALTH STRATEGIES

Journaling works best as part of a holistic approach to mental health. Combine it with other strategies for maximum benefit:

1. **Exercise**: After a workout, journal about how your body feels and how the activity affected your mood.
2. **Meditation**: Use your journal to reflect on your meditation experience or to further explore thoughts that arose during your practice.
3. **Cognitive Behavioral Therapy (CBT)**: Your journal becomes a place to practice CBT techniques, such as challenging negative thoughts or tracking behavior changes.
4. **Medication**: If you're taking medication for mental health, use your journal to track its effects, both positive and negative.

SAFETY PLANNING AND CRISIS JOURNALING

While journaling is a powerful tool, it's important to have a safety plan for moments of crisis. Work with your therapist or a trusted support person to develop this plan. Include emergency contact numbers, coping strategies, and reasons to stay alive.

In moments of intense distress, your journal can serve as a lifeline. Develop a specific crisis journaling template. This could include grounding exercises, affirmations, and reminders of your safety plan.

Sample crisis journal entry:

"I'm struggling right now. The pain feels unbearable. But I've survived this before. I will get through this again. I am breathing. I am safe in this moment. I choose to stay. I choose to reach out.

Name three people you can call:

1. [Trusted friend's name and number].

2. [Therapist's number]
3. [Crisis Hotline Number]

Remember: If you're thinking about hurting yourself or committing suicide, get help right away. Your life does matter.

THE JOURNEY CONTINUES

Journaling for mental health is not a linear journey. Some days the words will come easily. Other days, you may struggle to write a single sentence. Both of these experiences are valid and valuable.

Be patient with yourself. Healing and growth take time. Your journal is a witness to your journey, a testament to your resilience. Each entry, no matter how short or messy, is an act of self-care and courage.

As you continue this practice, you'll develop a deeper understanding of yourself. You'll discover strengths you didn't know you had. You'll find new ways to deal with life's challenges. And most importantly, you'll cultivate a kinder, more compassionate relationship with yourself.

Your journal is a powerful ally on your mental health journey. It's a place to explore, heal, and grow. It's a reminder that your story is still being written, and you hold the pen. Keep writing, keep reflecting, keep growing. Your future self will thank you for the insight and healing you're cultivating now, one page at a time.

TEN
THE INTERSECTION OF JOURNALING AND MEDITATION: MINDFUL WRITING PRACTICES

In the quiet space between thoughts, where meditation and journaling meet, a powerful synergy emerges. This chapter explores the deep connection between these two practices and offers techniques for deepening your self-awareness and cultivating inner peace through mindful writing.

THE MINDFULNESS-JOURNALING CONNECTION

Mindfulness, the practice of present-moment awareness without judgment, is the cornerstone of many meditation techniques. When applied to journaling, it transforms the act of writing into a meditative experience. This union amplifies the benefits of both practices, fostering greater self-understanding, emotional regulation, and overall well-being.

Research backs up this powerful combination. A study published in the Journal of Psychology found that participants who engaged in mindful journaling reported lower stress levels and increased self-compassion compared to those who practiced traditional journaling or meditation alone.

CREATE YOUR MINDFUL JOURNALING SPACE

To begin your mindful journaling practice, create an environment that is conducive to both writing and meditation. Choose a quiet, comfortable space that is free of distractions. Soft lighting, a supportive chair, and a clean writing surface set the stage for focused introspection.

Consider incorporating elements that engage your senses: a scented candle, a soft blanket, or a small plant. These sensory anchors can help ground you in the present moment as you write.

Prepare your journaling materials with intention. Choose a journal and pen that you enjoy using. The tactile experience of writing becomes part of the mindful practice.

BREATHING EXERCISES: THE GATEWAY TO MINDFUL WRITING

Before putting pen to paper, center yourself with a short breathing exercise. This transition helps shift your mind from the busyness of daily life to a more contemplative state.

Try this simple technique:

1. Sit comfortably with your feet flat on the floor and your hands in your lap.
2. Close your eyes and take three deep breaths, focusing on the sensation of air moving in and out of your body.
3. Allow your breathing to settle into its natural rhythm.
4. For the next minute, simply observe your breath without trying to change it.
5. If thoughts arise, acknowledge them without judgment and gently bring your focus back to your breath.
6. Slowly open your eyes and maintain this sense of calm awareness as you prepare to write.

This short meditation creates a mindful foundation for your journaling session.

THE BODY SCAN JOURNALING TECHNIQUE

The body scan, a cornerstone of many mindfulness practices, can be powerfully integrated into your journaling routine. This technique cultivates body awareness and helps you identify areas of tension or emotion that you might otherwise miss.

To practice body scan journaling:

1. Begin with the breathing exercise described above.
2. Beginning with your toes, bring your attention to each part of your body, moving upward.
3. As you focus on each area, write down any sensations, emotions, or thoughts you notice.
4. Be descriptive but not judgmental. Simply observe and record.

Example:

"My toes feel cool against the ground. Slight tension in my calves, like a rubber band being stretched. Warmth in my stomach - nervous about the upcoming presentation? Shoulders hunched, jaw clenched. Take a deep breath and let my shoulders drop. Notice a headache forming at my temples..."

This practice often reveals insights into your emotional and physical state, providing rich material for further reflection.

STREAM OF CONSCIOUSNESS: MEDITATION IN MOTION

Stream of consciousness writing serves as a form of active meditation, allowing thoughts and emotions to flow freely onto the page without censorship or judgment. This technique can be especially helpful for processing complex emotions or untangling mental knots.

To practice:

1. Set a timer for 10-15 minutes.
2. Start writing whatever comes to mind, without stopping to edit or revise.
3. If you get stuck, just write "I don't know what to write" until new thoughts come up.
4. Keep your pen moving, even if you're writing nonsense or repetition.
5. When the timer sounds, take a few deep breaths before reading what you've written.

This practice often brings unconscious thoughts and feelings to the surface, providing valuable insight and emotional release.

ZEN WRITING PRACTICES

Zen philosophy emphasizes direct experience and present-moment awareness. Incorporating Zen principles into your journaling can lead to profound insights and a deeper connection to your true self.

Try these Zen-inspired journaling exercises:

1. **Haiku journaling**: Capture your present experience in the traditional 5-7-5 syllable format of haiku. This concise form encourages careful observation and distillation of experience.

Example:

- Pen scratches paper
- Thoughts blossom like spring flowers
- Silence speaks volumes

2. Koan Contemplation: Reflect on a Zen koan (a paradoxical statement or question) in your journal. Write down your initial reactions, then return to the koan periodically, noting how your understanding evolves.

Example koan: "What is the sound of a hand clapping?"

3. Mindful description: Choose an object in your environment and describe it in minute detail as if you were seeing it for the first time. This practice sharpens your powers of observation and grounds you in the present moment.

LOVING-KINDNESS MEDITATION JOURNALING

Loving kindness meditation, also known as metta, cultivates feelings of goodwill toward oneself and others. Integrating this practice with journaling can increase self-compassion and improve relationships.

To practice:

1. Begin with a few minutes of loving-kindness meditation, silently repeating phrases such as "May I be happy. May I be healthy. May I be safe. May I live with ease.
2. Extend these wishes to others: a loved one, a neutral person, someone you find difficult, and finally all beings.
3. Open your journal and write a letter to yourself from this place of loving-kindness. What words of compassion and encouragement would you offer?
4. Next, write short notes to the others you have included in your meditation. You don't have to send them; the act of writing is the practice itself.

This exercise often reveals areas where you can cultivate greater compassion for yourself and others.

MINDFUL OBSERVATION JOURNALING

Sharpen your awareness of the present moment through mindful observation journaling. This practice encourages you to fully engage with your environment using all of your senses.

Try this exercise:

1. Find a comfortable place, either indoors or outdoors.
2. For five minutes, simply observe your surroundings without writing.
3. Open your journal and describe what you've observed using all five senses.
4. Challenge yourself to notice details that you might normally overlook.
5. As you write, maintain a sense of curiosity and wonder, as if you were experiencing everything for the first time.

Example:

"Sunlight dapples the wooden floor, creating ever-changing patterns. A light breeze carries the scent of jasmine through the open window. In the distance, wind chimes sing a delicate melody. The smooth paper beneath my fingers grounds me in this moment..."

This practice not only enhances your ability to observe, but also cultivates a deeper appreciation for the richness of everyday experience.

INTEGRATING MINDFUL JOURNALING INTO DAILY LIFE

The true power of mindful journaling comes when it is integrated into your daily life. Here are strategies for weaving this practice into your routine:

1. Morning pages: Write three stream-of-consciousness pages upon waking. This practice, popularized by Julia Cameron, clears mental clutter and sets a mindful tone for the day.
2. Mindful transitions: Use short journaling sessions to transition between activities. Take five minutes to check in with yourself and note your current state of mind and body.
3. Gratitude Pauses: Throughout the day, pause to record

moments of gratitude. This practice focuses your attention on the positive aspects of your experience.

4. Evening Reflection: Before bed, spend a few minutes reflecting on your day. Note moments of mindfulness and areas where you'd like to be more mindful.

OVERCOMING CHALLENGES TO MINDFUL WRITING

As with any practice, mindful journaling has its challenges. Common obstacles include:

1. Monkey mind: When your thoughts go off in all directions, gently bring your attention back to your breath or the physical sensation of writing.
2. Self-judgment: Notice when your inner critic comes up. Acknowledge these thoughts without attachment, then return to the present moment.
3. Expectations: Release expectations of what your practice "should" look like. Each session is unique and valuable, regardless of what appears on the page.
4. Consistency: If you miss a day, just start again. Treat yourself with compassion and remember that the practice is always available to you.

ADVANCED MINDFUL JOURNALING TECHNIQUES

As you deepen your practice, explore these advanced techniques:

1. Dialogue with Your Wisdom Self: Engage in a written dialogue with your higher self or inner wisdom. Ask questions and allow the answers to flow onto the page.
2. Chakra Journaling: Focus on each of the seven major chakras and write about the associated emotions, physical sensations, and life areas. This practice can reveal energetic imbalances and areas for growth.

3. Mindful Goal Setting: Approach goal setting from a place of mindful awareness. Rather than focusing solely on results, explore your deeper motivations and the person you want to become through the process of working toward your goals.

4. Shadow work: Use your journal to explore aspects of yourself that you typically avoid or repress. Approach this practice with self-compassion and consider working with a therapist when challenging emotions arise.

THE ONGOING JOURNEY

Mindful journaling is not a destination, but an ongoing journey of self-discovery and growth. As you continue the practice, you'll likely find that your writing becomes more reflective, your self-awareness deepens, and your capacity for presence in daily life expands.

Remember, there is no "perfect" way to practice mindful journaling. The practice is as unique as you are. Approach each session with curiosity and openness, and allow your experience to unfold naturally.

Your journal becomes a mirror, reflecting your inner landscape with increasing clarity. It's a trusted companion on your journey to greater mindfulness and self-understanding. With every mindful word you write, you cultivate a deeper connection to yourself and the world around you.

So pick up your pen, take a deep breath, and begin. The present moment is waiting, ready to reveal its wisdom on the pages of your journal.

ELEVEN
JOURNALING THROUGH CHRONIC ILLNESS: COPING STRATEGIES AND HEALTH TRACKING

T he blank page stares back at you, a silent witness to your struggle. Living with chronic illness often feels like navigating an ever-changing landscape, but your journal can become a steadfast companion on this unpredictable journey. This chapter explores how journaling can empower you to manage your health, process complex emotions, and find moments of light even during the darkest days.

THE ROLE OF JOURNALING IN CHRONIC ILLNESS MANAGEMENT

Chronic illness is disruptive. It challenges our sense of self, strains relationships, and requires constant adjustment. In the midst of this turmoil, journaling provides a powerful anchor. It provides a space to track symptoms, identify patterns, and make sense of your experiences. More than just a record, your journal becomes a tool for self-advocacy and a source of valuable insights for you and your healthcare team.

Research supports the effectiveness of journaling for people living with chronic conditions. A study published in the Journal of Pain and Symptom Management found that patients who engaged in expressive writing experienced reduced pain intensity and improved physical functioning compared to a control group.

SETTING UP YOUR HEALTH JOURNALING SYSTEM

Creating an effective health journaling system requires thoughtful preparation. Consider these elements:

1. Choose your medium: A paper journal offers tactile engagement and freedom from screens, while a digital platform offers searchability and data analysis tools. Some find that a hybrid approach works best.
2. Establish a routine: Set aside time each day to journal, even if it's just five minutes. Consistency is more important than length.
3. Decide on your format: Will you use free writing, structured templates, or a combination? Experiment to see what works best for you.
4. Gather supplies: Keep your journal, pen, and any additional materials (symptom trackers, medication lists) easily accessible.

Remember, your journaling system should serve you, not become another source of stress. Start simple and adjust as needed.

SYMPTOM TRACKING AND PATTERN RECOGNITION

Consistent symptom tracking is the backbone of effective health journaling. It provides valuable data for both you and your healthcare providers. Here's how to get started:

1. Create a symptom log: Record the type, intensity, duration, and possible triggers of your symptoms. Use a numerical scale (1-10) for pain or other measurable experiences.

2. Note environmental factors: Track weather conditions, stress levels, diet, and activity patterns along with your symptoms.
3. Be specific: Instead of simply writing "fatigue," describe it in detail. "Exhaustion so severe that I can barely lift my arms. Even thinking feels like wading through molasses."
4. Look for patterns: Review your entries periodically. Do certain symptoms cluster? Are there correlations with certain activities or times of day?

Example entry:

"Date: 5/15/2023

Pain level: 7/10 (sharp, stabbing pain in lower back)

Fatigue: 8/10 (struggled to get out of bed, needed a nap by 2 pm)

Weather: Rainy, barometric pressure dropped significantly

Diet: Skipped breakfast, ate coffee and toast for lunch

Notes: Stress at work - big project deadline tomorrow

Over time, these entries can provide invaluable insight into your condition and possible management strategies.

PAIN JOURNALING TECHNIQUES

For many people with chronic conditions, pain becomes an unwelcome constant. Journaling about pain can help you better understand and communicate your experience. Try these techniques:

1. Body mapping: Draw an outline of your body and color in areas where you experience pain. Use different colors to represent different intensities or types of pain.
2. Pain descriptors: Make a list of words to describe your pain (throbbing, burning, aching, etc.). Use these consistently in

your entries to track how the quality of your pain changes over time.

3. Impact assessment: Write about how the pain affects your daily activities, mood, and relationships. This information can be important for treatment planning.
4. Coping strategies log: Document pain management techniques you've tried and their effectiveness. Include both medical interventions and self-care practices.

Example:

"The pain radiates from my lower back, tendrils of fire snaking down my legs. Sitting makes it worse, forcing me to cancel dinner plans with friends. I tried deep breathing exercises - minimal relief. The ice pack provided temporary numbness, but the pain returned with a vengeance. Tomorrow I'll try gentle stretching, if the pain allows."

MEDICATION AND TREATMENT RECORDS

Keeping track of medications, treatments, and their effects is critical to managing chronic conditions. Your diary can serve as a comprehensive record:

1. Create a medication list: Include dosages, frequency, starting dates, and any noted side effects.
2. Track compliance: Note any missed doses and the reasons why.
3. Record treatment responses: Document how you feel after treatments or medication changes. Be specific about any improvements or new symptoms.
4. Write down questions for your healthcare team: Write down any concerns or questions as they arise so you don't forget to bring them up at your next appointment.

This detailed record will help you have more productive conversations with your healthcare providers and make informed decisions about your treatment plan.

EMOTIONAL PROCESSING AND COPING

Chronic disease takes an emotional toll. Your diary provides a safe space to explore and process these complex feelings:

1. **Emotional check-ins**: Regularly assess and write about your emotional state. Are you feeling frustrated, anxious, hopeful, or resigned?
2. **Worry Dump**: Set a timer for 5 minutes and write down all your worries without censoring them. Often, seeing them on paper can make them feel more manageable.
3. **Reframing exercise**: Challenge negative thoughts by writing down alternative perspectives. For example, "I'm useless because I can't work" could become "I'm finding new ways to contribute and find meaning beyond traditional work."
4. **Strength Spotting**: Identify and write about moments of resilience, no matter how small. Celebrate the ways you cope and adapt to your circumstances.

Example:

"Today I am overwhelmed with frustration. This flare-up has been going on for weeks, and I'm tired of canceling plans and disappointing people. But I did manage to take a shower and cook a simple meal. These small victories count. I'm still here, still fighting. Maybe tomorrow will be better."

GRATITUDE AND POSITIVITY PRACTICES

While toxic positivity should be avoided, cultivating genuine gratitude can have a significant impact on your well-being. Try these practices:

1. Daily gratitude: List three things you're grateful for each day, no matter how small.
2. Silver Linings Journal: For every challenge you face, try to identify one positive aspect or lesson learned.
3. Joy Spotting: Make a conscious effort to notice and record moments of joy, however fleeting.
4. Future Self Visualization: Write a letter to your future self, imagining a time when you've learned to thrive despite your illness.

These practices can help shift your focus from what your illness has taken away to what is still possible.

COMMUNICATING WITH HEALTH CARE PROVIDERS

Your journal becomes a powerful tool for advocating for yourself in medical settings:

1. Prepare for appointments: Review your journal entries before visits, noting key symptoms, concerns, and questions.
2. Summarize data: Create concise summaries of symptom patterns or treatment responses to share with your providers.
3. Document conversations: After appointments, record key points discussed, treatment plans, and any follow-up steps.
4. Track test results: Keep a log of important lab or imaging results, noting any significant changes over time.

By presenting clear, detailed information, you become an active partner in your health care decisions.

SETTING GOALS AND TRACKING PROGRESS

Chronic illness may change the trajectory of your life, but it doesn't eliminate the possibility of growth and achievement. Use your diary to set adaptive goals:

1. Set SMART goals: Specific, Measurable, Achievable, Relevant, and Time-Bound goals that take into account your current health status.
2. Break goals down into manageable steps: Big goals can feel overwhelming. Break them down into smaller, achievable tasks.
3. Celebrate progress: Acknowledge every step forward, no matter how small it may seem.
4. Evaluate and adjust: Review your goals regularly and adjust them as needed based on your health and circumstances.

Example:

Goal: "Increase my endurance to sit through my son's entire soccer game.

Step 1: Practice sitting upright for 15 minutes twice a day.

Step 2: Attend one game for 15 minutes, then gradually increase time

Step 3: Use mobility aids or adaptive seating as needed

Time frame: Aim for full game attendance within 2 months"

BALANCING HONESTY AND HOPE

Your journal should be a place of truth as well as possibility. Aim for balance:

1. Acknowledge struggles: Be honest about your struggles and limitations. Suppressing these feelings often backfires.
2. Cultivate hope: Along with challenges, write about your hopes, dreams, and opportunities for the future.
3. Focus on what you can control: Write about actions you can take to improve your situation, no matter how small.
4. Practice self-compassion: Use your journal to speak to yourself with kindness and understanding.

Remember that it's possible to be both realistic about your circumstances and hopeful about your ability to find meaning and joy in them.

ACCEPTANCE AND RESILIENCE JOURNALING EXERCISES

Acceptance doesn't mean giving up. It means acknowledging reality while choosing how to respond. Try these exercises:

1. Letter about your illness: Write a letter expressing your feelings about your illness. What has it taken from you? What has it taught you?
2. Values Clarification: Think about what is most important to you. How can you honor these values in the context of your illness?
3. Resilience inventory: List the challenges you've overcome and the strengths you've developed through living with chronic illness.
4. Adaptation stories: Write about times when you've successfully adapted to health-related limitations. How can these inform future challenges?

These exercises can help you develop a more flexible, resilient mindset in the face of ongoing health challenges.

CREATING A SUPPORT NETWORK THROUGH SHARED JOURNALING

While your personal journal remains private, shared journaling experiences can provide valuable support:

1. Join a journaling group for people with chronic illness.
2. Start a blog to connect with others who are facing similar challenges.
3. Collaborate on a journal with a trusted friend or family member to improve communication and understanding.

Sharing your experiences can reduce isolation and provide new perspectives on living with chronic illness.

CONCLUSION: YOUR DIARY AS A COMPANION

Living with chronic illness can often feel like an isolating journey, but your journal can become a constant companion. It witnesses your struggles, celebrates your victories, and helps you make sense of the complex terrain of living with ongoing health challenges.

Through consistent journaling, you develop a deeper understanding of your body, your disease, and yourself. You will cultivate resilience, self-advocacy skills, and the ability to find moments of light even in the darkest days.

Remember, there's no "right" way to journal through chronic illness. Your practice will evolve as your needs and health status change. Be patient with yourself, write with honesty and compassion, and trust in the healing power of putting your experiences into words.

Your journal is more than a record of your illness; it's a testament to your strength, adaptability, and perseverance. Keep writing, keep fighting, and keep hope alive - one page at a time.

TWELVE
JOURNALING FOR SOCIAL CHANGE: DOCUMENTING AND REFLECTING ON ACTIVISM AND COMMUNITY ENGAGEMENT

The pen trembles in your hand, poised over the blank page. Around you, voices rise in protest, signs wave in the air, and the energy of collective action pulses through the crowd. How do you capture this moment, this movement? Your journal becomes more than a personal record; it transforms into a tool for social change, a witness to history in the making.

UNDERSTANDING THE POWER OF PERSONAL NARRATIVES IN SOCIAL MOVEMENTS

Throughout history, personal narratives have fueled social movements. From Anne Frank's diary that illuminated the horrors of the Holocaust to the slave narratives that galvanized the abolitionist movement, individual stories have the power to humanize issues and inspire action.

Your journal, filled with your observations, reflections, and experiences, contributes to this tradition. It offers a ground-level view of social change, providing context and emotional resonance to complement broader historical accounts.

SETTING UP YOUR ACTIVIST JOURNAL

Before you get started, consider how to structure your activist journal:

1. Choose a durable, portable notebook or secure digital platform.
2. Create sections for different types of entries: event documentation, personal reflections, ideas for action, and resources.
3. Develop a system for taking notes quickly during events (shorthand, symbols, sketches).
4. Include a contact section for other activists and organizations.

Remember that your activist journal serves multiple purposes: documenting events, processing your experiences, and planning future actions. Structure it to support all of these functions.

DOCUMENTING PROTESTS, MEETINGS, AND COMMUNITY EVENTS

When you're in the midst of action, focus on recording key details:

- Date, time, and location
- Estimated crowd size
- Key messages and demands
- Speakers and their main points
- Police presence and interactions
- Notable incidents or turning points

Example entry:

"June 15, 2023 - Climate March, City Hall Plaza

~5000 protesters

Chants: "Climate Justice Now!" "No Planet B!"

Speaker Highlight: Dr. Jane Chen - "We have 7 years to cut emissions in half".

Police present but peaceful. One arrest when protester climbed flagpole".

Key moment: Mayor appeared to address crowd, promised to present Green New Deal to City Council next week.

Include sketches or photos if possible, but be aware of privacy concerns. Your detailed accounts may prove valuable for future organizing or legal purposes.

REFLECTION TECHNIQUES FOR ADDRESSING SOCIAL ISSUES

After the action subsides, deeper reflection begins. Use these techniques to process what you've experienced:

1. Free writing: Set a timer for 10 minutes and write continuously about the event, allowing your thoughts and feelings to flow uncensored.
2. Structured reflection: Answer specific questions such as

   - What surprised me about the event?
   - How did it challenge or strengthen my beliefs?
   - What questions or doubts arose?

1. Dialogue Writing: Create a conversation between different perspectives on the issue, exploring different points of view.
2. Visual mapping: Draw connections between different aspects of the issue, creating a visual representation of its complexity.

Example Reflection:

"The Climate March left me both energized and overwhelmed. I was inspired by the creativity of the youth marchers-their signs, their chants, their unwa-

vering conviction. But I can't shake the feeling of fear. Are we too late? How do we turn this energy into real political change? I need to learn more about local initiatives..."

USING JOURNALING TO CLARIFY YOUR VALUES AND GOALS IN ACTIVISM

Your journal provides a space to explore your motivations and refine your focus:

1. **Values inventory**: List your core values and reflect on how they relate to your activism.
2. **Goal Setting**: Use the SMART framework (Specific, Measurable, Achievable, Relevant, Time-bound) to set personal activist goals.
3. **Role Exploration**: Write about different roles you might play in the movement. Where do your skills and passions align with the needs of the cause?
4. **Ethical Dilemmas**: Use your journal to work through difficult ethical questions you encounter in your activism.

Example:

"My core values: Justice, Compassion, Sustainability

How they relate to my climate activism:

- *Justice: Fighting for those most affected by climate change*
- *Compassion: Extending empathy to all beings, including future generations*
- *Sustainability: Promoting practices that balance human needs with ecological limits"*

GOAL: ORGANIZE A COMMUNITY WORKSHOP ON REDUCING HOUSEHOLD carbon footprints within the next 3 months.

Steps:

1. Research effective carbon reduction strategies
2. Connect with local environmental groups for assistance
3. Secure a venue and set a date
4. Develop workshop content and materials
5. Promote the event through social media and community networks".

STRATEGIES FOR STAYING ENERGIZED AND AVOIDING BURNOUT

Activism takes a lot out of you. Use your journal to monitor your well-being and prevent burnout:

1. Regular check-ins: Schedule weekly reflections on your emotional and physical state.
2. Practice gratitude: Write down moments of progress, connection, or inspiration to keep you motivated.
3. Boundary Setting: Use your journal to explore and set healthy boundaries in your activist work.
4. Self-care planning: Brainstorm and plan activities that rejuvenate you.

Example entry:

"Feeling exhausted after three straight weeks of action. Need to step back and recharge. This weekend: no phone, long hike in the woods, socializing with non-activist friends. Remember, self-care is not selfish. I can't pour from an empty cup."

COMMUNITY JOURNALING FOR COMMUNITY ORGANIZING

While personal journaling remains crucial, collaborative journaling can enhance community organizing efforts:

1. **Shared digital platforms**: Use tools like Google Docs or Notion for collaborative planning and reflection.
2. **Circle journals**: Pass a physical journal among group members, with each person adding entries before passing it on.
3. **Collaborative art journals**: Create visual representations of your movement's journey and goals.

These shared journals foster connection, align goals, and create a collective memory of your movement's evolution.

TURN JOURNAL ENTRIES INTO OP-EDS, BLOG POSTS, OR SPEECHES

Your personal reflections can become powerful public statements. To turn journal entries into shareable content

1. Identify powerful anecdotes or insights in your entries.
2. Develop a clear thesis statement or call to action.
3. Support your argument with facts and data that complement your personal narrative.
4. Edit for clarity and impact while maintaining your authentic voice.

Example: A journal entry about a conversation with a climate change denier could become an op-ed about the importance of empathetic communication in addressing the climate crisis.

ETHICAL CONSIDERATIONS WHEN DOCUMENTING SOCIAL MOVEMENTS

As you document your experiences, consider the ethical implications:

1. Protect privacy: Use pseudonyms or general descriptions for people who haven't agreed to be identified.
2. Examine your biases: Think about how your background and

beliefs might influence your perceptions and try to present balanced accounts.

3. Be aware of sensitive information: Consider the potential consequences of losing or confiscating your journal.
4. Respect different tactics: Even if you disagree with certain approaches, strive to document them objectively.

Example reflection:

"I am struggling with how to write about today's action. The property damage goes against my beliefs in nonviolent protest, but I understand the frustration behind it. How can I honestly document this without delegitimizing the broader goals of the movement?"

JOURNALING EXERCISES FOR DEVELOPING EMPATHY AND UNDERSTANDING DIVERSE PERSPECTIVES

Use your journal to expand your understanding and challenge your assumptions:

1. **Perspective Taking**: Write from the perspective of someone with a different point of view on your topic. What are their concerns and motivations?
2. **Interview reflections:** After talking with different stakeholders, write about what you learned and how it changed your perspective.
3. **Media Analysis**: Compare coverage of the events you witnessed across news sources. Reflect on the biases and framing you observe.
4. **Historical connections**: Research and write about historical parallels to current movements. What lessons can you apply?

Example Exercise:

"Today I'm writing from the perspective of a worker in the factory our campaign is targeting. What are their fears about our demands for sustain-

ability measures? How might job insecurity affect their view of our movement?"

USING YOUR JOURNAL TO TRACK THE IMPACT OF YOUR ACTIVISM

Your journal will become a record of your movement's progress:

1. **Milestone tracking**: Note key victories, setbacks, and turning points.
2. **Personal growth**: Reflect on how your skills, knowledge, and network have grown through your activism.
3. **Ripple Effects**: Document any unexpected outcomes or impacts of your work.
4. **Long-term visioning**: Periodically write about your vision for the future. How has it evolved?

Example entry:

"One year since the launch of our campaign. Victories:

- *City Council passed a resolution supporting our requests.*
- *Membership tripled*
- *Two local businesses adopted our suggested practices*

Challenges:

- *Counter-movement gaining traction*
- *Funding still tight*
- *Core team showing signs of burnout"*

Next steps: Need to focus on sustainable growth and building broader coalitions."

From the personal to the political: Connecting individual experiences to broader social issues

Your journal is a bridge between the personal and the political. Use it to explore those connections:

1. **Impact mapping**: How do broader issues directly impact your life and community?
2. **Privilege Examination**: Reflect on how your identities impact your experiences and activism.
3. **Exploring connections**: Draw connections between different social issues. How do they intersect and influence one another?
4. **Personal-Political Integration**: How has your activism changed your daily life and relationships?

Example reflection:

"I realized today how deeply the fear of climate change is affecting my decision to have children. This isn't just a global issue; it's deeply personal. How many others are struggling with this? How do we address the emotional toll of activism without losing the urgency?"

CONCLUSION: YOUR JOURNAL AS A CATALYST FOR CHANGE

Your activist journal is more than a record; it's a revolutionary act. Through consistent documentation and reflection, you sharpen your understanding, refine your strategies, and amplify your impact. Your personal stories, when shared, have the power to move hearts and change minds.

As you continue your journey of activism and journaling, remember:

1. Your experiences matter. Your on-the-ground observations provide critical context for broader narratives.
2. Reflection fuels action. Regular journaling helps you process, strategize, and sustain your commitment.
3. Personal growth and social change are intertwined. When you work to change the world, you inevitably change yourself.

4. Your words have power. Today's journal entry could be tomorrow's rallying cry.

Keep writing, keep thinking, keep acting. Your journal is both a witness to history and a tool for shaping it. In your hands, the pen is truly mightier than the sword.

THIRTEEN
ECO-JOURNALING: SUSTAINABLE PRACTICES AND ENVIRONMENTAL AWARENESS IN JOURNALING

The crisp pages of your journal rustle as a gentle breeze sweeps through the forest. You pause, pen hovering above the paper, and breathe in the earthy scent of pine and damp earth. This moment, this connection to nature, deserves to be captured. But how can your journaling practice itself reflect the environmental values you hold dear?

Eco-journaling combines the introspective power of writing with a deep awareness of our place in the natural world. It's not just about what you write, but how you write it. Every choice, from the materials you use to the way you observe your surroundings, becomes an act of environmental stewardship.

CHOOSING ENVIRONMENTALLY FRIENDLY JOURNALING SUPPLIES

Your journey into eco-journaling begins with the tools you choose. Consider the life cycle of each item:

1. **Journals**: Choose journals made from recycled paper or alternative fibers such as bamboo or hemp. Look for

certifications such as FSC (Forest Stewardship Council) to ensure responsible sourcing.

2. **Pens and pencils**: Look for refillable pens to reduce plastic waste. Wood pencils from sustainably managed forests or mechanical pencils with recyclable lead refills are environmentally friendly alternatives.
3. **Inks**: Look for plant-based inks or make your own using natural pigments such as berries or tea.
4. **Supplies**: Choose biodegradable washi tape, paper clips made from recycled materials, and bookmarks made from upcycled fabrics.

Example reflection:

"When I hold this hemp-paper journal, I'm struck by its texture-slightly rough, a tangible reminder of its natural origins. The bamboo pen feels light in my hand, a stark contrast to the heavy weight of environmental responsibility. Every word I write becomes a small act of environmentally conscious choice".

TECHNIQUES FOR REDUCING WASTE IN YOUR JOURNALING PRACTICE

Mindful consumption goes beyond the initial purchase. Incorporate these waste reduction strategies into your practice:

1. **Use every inch**: Fill pages completely before starting a new journal. Write in smaller type or experiment with different page layouts to maximize space.
2. **Upcycle**: Turn old books or magazines into junk journals. Cut up used envelopes or packaging to create unique collage elements.
3. **Digital integration:** For information you need to refer to frequently, consider keeping digital notes to reduce paper consumption.

4. **Repair and Maintain**: Learn basic bookbinding techniques to extend the life of cherished journals.
5. **Compost**: When your journal is truly at the end of its life, compost the paper components (removing any non-biodegradable elements first).

NATURE JOURNALING: CONNECTING WITH AND DOCUMENTING THE ENVIRONMENT

Get outside and let the natural world be your muse. Nature journaling sharpens your observational skills and deepens your connection to the environment:

1. **Tracking phenology**: Document the seasonal changes in your local ecosystem. Note the first blooming of spring flowers, the arrival of migratory birds, or the changing colors of autumn leaves.
2. **Species identification**: Draw and describe the plants and animals you encounter. Use field guides to learn their names and ecological roles.
3. **Sensory Observation**: Use all your senses. Record the sounds of birdsong, the scent of rain-soaked earth, the texture of tree bark.
4. **Weather Patterns**: Keep track of local weather conditions and how they affect the landscape and wildlife around you.

Example entry:

"April 15: The trillium I've been watching unfurled its three-petaled flower today. White as fresh snow, with a hint of pink in the center. A bumblebee, its pollen baskets heavy with yellow dust, buzzed lazily from flower to flower. The forest floor came alive, a patchwork of green and white against the rich, dark soil."

TRACKING PERSONAL ECOLOGICAL IMPACT THROUGH JOURNALING

Your journal becomes a powerful tool for self-reflection and account-ability on your environmental journey:

1. **Carbon footprint journal**: Document your daily activities and associated carbon emissions. Explore the impact of different choices and brainstorm ways to reduce your footprint.
2. **Consumption Log**: Track your purchases, noting packaging materials and product life cycles. Think about needs versus wants.
3. **Waste Audit**: Track the waste you generate over a period of time. Categorize it and identify areas for reduction.
4. **Energy Use**: Monitor your home's energy use and brainstorm conservation strategies.

Example entry:

"Weekly waste audit results:

- *Recycling: 2 pounds (mostly paper and cardboard)*
- *Compost: 3 lbs (food scraps and yard waste)*
- *Landfill: 1.5 lbs (plastic packaging, non-recyclable items)"*

Reflection: Plastic packaging continues to be my biggest challenge. Next week's goal: Research local bulk food options to reduce reliance on packaged goods. Can I realistically cut my landfill waste in half?

REFLECTION EXERCISES ON SUSTAINABILITY AND LIFESTYLE CHOICES

Use your journal to take a deeper look at your environmental values and choices:

1. Values Clarification: List your most important environmental values. How do your daily actions align (or conflict) with these values?
2. Habit Tracker: Create a chart to track the green habits you're trying to develop (e.g., using reusable bags, taking shorter showers).
3. Ethical Dilemmas: Explore complex environmental issues in writing. Consider multiple perspectives and research different solutions.
4. Visioning exercises: Describe in vivid detail your ideal sustainable future. What steps can you take to move toward this vision?

Example reflection:

"I value biodiversity, but I've never really considered the impact of my diet on ecosystems. Research shows that animal agriculture is a leading cause of habitat destruction. Can I align my eating habits more closely with my values? What would a transition to a plant-based diet look like for me? Challenges: Family traditions, convenience. Benefits: Reduced environmental impact, potential health improvements. Next step: Start with one plant-based day a week and journal about the experience."

USE YOUR JOURNAL TO PLAN AND TRACK GREEN INITIATIVES

Turn your reflections into action:

1. Set goals: Use the SMART framework (Specific, Measurable, Achievable, Relevant, Time-bound) to set environmental goals.
2. Project Planning: Outline steps for green projects, whether personal (planting a garden) or community-based (organizing a neighborhood cleanup).
3. Track progress: Regularly review and update your goals, celebrate successes, and adjust strategies as needed.

4. Collect resources: Compile lists of helpful books, Web sites, and local organizations related to your environmental interests.

Example entry:

"Project: Reduce household water use

Goal: Reduce water consumption by 20% over the next 3 months.

Action Steps:

1. *Install low-flow showerheads and faucet aerators (Week 1)*
2. *Fix leaky toilet (Week 2)*
3. *Research and implement gray water system for garden irrigation (Weeks 3-6)*
4. *Track water bills to measure progress*
5. *Educate family members about water conservation techniques*

Resources:

- Local water conservation office for free low-flow fixtures
- The Water-Wise Home book for graywater system ideas
- Water Sense website for additional tips

GRATITUDE PRACTICES FOCUSED ON NATURE AND THE ENVIRONMENT

Cultivate an appreciation for the natural world:

1. Daily appreciation of nature: Each day, write about one aspect of nature for which you're grateful, from the grand (a stunning sunset) to the minute (the intricate pattern of a leaf).
2. Reflect on ecosystem services: Research and journal about the often-overlooked ways nature supports human life (e.g., air purification by trees, soil fertilization by earthworms).

3. Outdoor Meditation: Combine mindfulness practices with nature appreciation. Sit quietly outdoors and then journal about the experience.
4. Biomimicry Inspiration: Reflect on how nature's designs can inspire sustainable solutions to human challenges.

Sample entry:

"I am grateful for the spider weaving its web outside my window. I am inspired by its silken architecture, both delicate and strong. Nature's engineer, working tirelessly to create beauty and function. How can I emulate this balance of aesthetics and purpose in my own work?"

JOURNALING PROMPTS FOR EXPLORING ENVIRONMENTAL ETHICS AND PHILOSOPHY

Deepen your understanding of environmental issues:

1. Examine your personal environmental philosophy. What do terms like "sustainability," "conservation," and "stewardship" mean to you?
2. Think about the concept of environmental justice. How do environmental issues intersect with social and economic inequalities?
3. Consider the rights of nature. Should ecosystems or species have legal rights? What would this look like in practice?
4. Examine your relationship to technology. How can technological advances help or hinder environmental protection?
5. Explore the tension between individual action and systemic change. What's the role of personal choices in addressing global environmental challenges?

Exploration Example:

"The concept of natural rights challenges my anthropocentric worldview. If a river had legal personality, how would that change our relationship with it? Would it lead to better protection or create unforeseen complications? I'm drawn to the idea of formally recognizing the intrinsic value of nature, but implementation seems complex. More research is needed on real-world examples like New Zealand's Whanganui River."

COMMUNITY ECO-JOURNALING PROJECTS AND IDEA SHARING

Extend your practice beyond individual reflection:

1. Start an eco-journaling group. Meet regularly to observe and document local ecosystems together.
2. Create a community phenology calendar. Work with neighbors to track seasonal changes in your area.
3. Organize a "green ideas" journal exchange. Share a journal with friends or colleagues, each adding green tips or reflections.
4. Participate in citizen science projects. Use your nature observations to support scientific research through platforms such as iNaturalist or eBird.

Example community project reflection:

"Our neighborhood phenology project is taking shape. Ten families have pledged to track spring blooms in their yards. We'll compile our observations into a local 'Signs of Spring' guide. I can already see the excitement growing - Sarah's kids are now eagerly awaiting the first robin sighting. This shared attention fosters a deeper collective connection to our local environment."

TRANSFORMING ENVIRONMENTAL ANXIETY INTO POSITIVE ACTION THROUGH WRITING

Eco-anxiety-the fear and worry about environmental degradation-is becoming increasingly common. Use your journal to process these feelings and channel them into constructive action:

1. Emotion mapping: Identify and name the specific emotions you're experiencing related to environmental issues.
2. Worry dump: Set a timer and write down all your environmental fears and concerns without censorship.
3. From anxiety to action: For each worry you've identified, brainstorm a concrete step you can take to address it, no matter how small.
4. Hope spotting: Actively seek out and document positive environmental news and success stories.
5. Self-care planning: Develop strategies to manage environmental anxiety, such as media breaks or time in nature.

Example anxiety-to-action entry:

"Feeling overwhelmed by news of biodiversity loss. Specific concern: Insect populations are declining worldwide.

Action step: Research native plants that support pollinators.

Next step: Convert part of lawn to wildflower meadow.

Reminder: Small actions matter. My meadow could be a butterfly's critical habitat."

CREATING A LONG-TERM VISION FOR PERSONAL AND GLOBAL SUSTAINABILITY

Use your journal to envision and work toward a sustainable future:

1. **Five-year sustainability plan**: Outline your personal environmental goals for the next five years. Be specific and ambitious.
2. **Future Scenario Building**: Describe several possible futures

based on different environmental outcomes. What might your life and society look like in each scenario?

3. **Legacy reflection**: Write a letter to future generations describing the environmental legacy you would like to leave.

4. **Backcasting**: Start with your ideal sustainable future and work backwards, detailing the steps needed to achieve that vision.

Example Vision Entry:

"Vision 2030: My home is a model of urban sustainability. Solar panels sparkle on the roof, powering not only my needs but also feeding excess power into the community grid. The front yard, once a monoculture of grass, now bursts with native plants, attracting a symphony of pollinators. Rainwater harvesting systems nourish the thriving vegetable garden, which provides most of my produce needs. Inside, every purchase is carefully considered for its environmental impact. I've found a deep satisfaction in this simpler, more connected way of life. The journey hasn't always been easy, but each step has brought me closer to my values. Looking ahead, I'm excited to share these practices with my community and create ripples of positive change."

CONCLUSION: CULTIVATING A LIFELONG ENVIRONMENTAL PRACTICE

Eco-journaling is more than a writing technique; it's a way of moving through the world with heightened awareness and intention. As you continue this practice, you'll likely find that your connection to the natural world deepens, your environmental knowledge expands, and your capacity for positive action grows.

Remember, the goal isn't perfection, but progress. Each entry, each observation, each moment of reflection is a step toward a more sustainable and harmonious relationship with our planet. Your journal will become both a record of your personal environmental journey and a tool for creating the change you wish to see in the world.

Keep writing, keep observing, keep questioning. The earth has many stories to tell, and through your eco-journal you become both listener and storyteller. Your words, rooted in mindful observation and thoughtful reflection, have the power to nurture the seeds of change - in yourself and in the world around you.

FOURTEEN
JOURNALING AND ARTIFICIAL INTELLIGENCE: ETHICAL CONSIDERATIONS AND FUTURE POSSIBILITIES

The cursor flashes on your screen, a digital heartbeat pulsing with potential. You hover your fingers over the keyboard, ready to begin your daily journaling session. But something's different this time. An AI writing assistant is waiting, ready to augment your thoughts, suggest prompts, or even analyze your entries for patterns and insights. Welcome to the frontier of AI-powered journaling, where technology and introspection intertwine in ways that are both exhilarating and unsettling.

INTRODUCTION TO AI IN THE CONTEXT OF PERSONAL WRITING

Artificial Intelligence has permeated nearly every aspect of our digital lives, and journaling is no exception. From simple autocomplete features to sophisticated language models capable of generating human-like text, AI offers a range of tools to enhance our writing experience. But what does it mean to invite an artificial entity into our most private thoughts and reflections?

AI in journaling can take many forms:

1. Writing assistants that offer suggestions as you type
2. Prompt generators that provide inspiration for entries
3. Sentiment analysis tools that track your mood over time
4. Pattern recognition algorithms that identify recurring themes in your writing
5. AI-powered journaling apps that can even interact with you about your entries.

As we explore these technologies, we must grapple with fundamental questions about the nature of personal expression, privacy, and the role of technology in our inner lives.

CURRENT AI TOOLS FOR JOURNALING AND WRITING ASSISTANCE

The landscape of AI writing tools is rapidly evolving. Here's an overview of some of the current offerings:

1. **GPT-based writing assistants**: These can help complete sentences, offer alternative phrases, or even generate entire paragraphs based on your input.
2. **Sentiment analysis tools**: Apps like Journify use natural language processing to track your emotional state across posts and provide visualizations of your mood over time.
3. **AI journaling prompts**: Websites and apps offer algorithmically generated prompts tailored to your interests or writing history.
4. **Personalized insights**: Some apps analyze your entries to provide observations about your habits, relationships, or personal growth.
5. **Voice-to-text with AI enhancement**: Dictate your entries and let AI clean up the transcription and even suggest edits.

Example interaction:

You: *"I'm feeling stuck today. I want to write about my career, but I'm not sure where to start."*

AI: *"Think about a recent challenge you faced at work. How did you handle it? What did you learn? Alternatively, you could explore your long-term career goals and the steps you might take to achieve them."*

ETHICAL CONSIDERATIONS IN USING AI FOR PERSONAL REFLECTION

As we invite AI into our journaling practice, we must confront a number of ethical issues:

1. Authenticity: Does AI assistance dilute the authenticity of our personal reflections?
2. Privacy: How can we ensure that our most intimate thoughts remain secure when shared with AI systems?
3. Dependence: Might we become overly reliant on AI for self-reflection, stunting our own capacity for introspection?
4. Bias: How do we address the potential for AI to perpetuate or reinforce biases in our thinking?
5. Ownership: Who owns the insights generated by AI analysis of our journal entries?

Reflection Exercise:

"I've been using an AI writing assistant for a week now. It's uncanny how it seems to anticipate my thoughts, sometimes offering insights I hadn't considered. But I wonder: are these really my thoughts, or am I being subtly influenced by the AI's suggestions? Does it matter if the end result is greater self-understanding? I'm both intrigued and uneasy."

TECHNIQUES FOR WORKING WITH AI IN YOUR JOURNALING PRACTICE

To take advantage of AI while maintaining the integrity of your personal practice, consider these approaches:

1. **Use AI as a conversation partner**: Engage with AI-generated prompts or insights as you would with a thoughtful friend, using them as a springboard for deeper reflection.
2. **Practice discernment**: Critically evaluate AI suggestions. Ask yourself why you're drawn to (or repelled by) certain ideas it offers.
3. **Maintain balance**: Alternate between AI-assisted and purely self-generated entries to maintain your authentic voice.
4. **Set boundaries**: Clearly define which aspects of your journaling practice you're comfortable augmenting with AI and which you prefer to keep tech-free.
5. **Review regularly**: Regularly assess how AI is impacting your journaling. Does it enhance or detract from your self-reflection?

USING AI FOR JOURNALING PROMPTS AND INSPIRATION

AI can be a powerful tool for overcoming writer's block and exploring new avenues of self-reflection:

1. **Topic-based prompts**: Enter a topic you'd like to explore and let AI generate specific questions or scenarios for you to write about.
2. **Style emulation**: Ask the AI to generate prompts in the style of your favorite authors or thinkers for a fresh perspective.
3. **What-if scenarios**: Use AI to create hypothetical situations that challenge your usual thinking patterns.
4. **Opposing viewpoints**: Let AI present arguments contrary to your usual stance on issues to stimulate critical thinking.
5. **Time Travel Prompts**: Request prompts that encourage you to write from the perspective of your past or future self.

Example AI-generated prompt:

"Imagine you could have a conversation with your 10-year-old self. What wisdom would you impart? What questions might your younger self ask that would make you rethink your current priorities?"

AI-ASSISTED ANALYSIS OF JOURNAL ENTRIES FOR INSIGHTS AND PATTERNS

One of the most powerful applications of AI in journaling is its ability to analyze large amounts of text to identify patterns and insights:

1. **Emotional trajectory**: Visualize how your mood fluctuates over time, correlating with events or themes in your entries.
2. **Recurring themes**: Identify issues or concerns that recur in your writing, perhaps revealing subconscious preoccupations.
3. **Language patterns**: Analyze changes in your vocabulary or sentence structure over time, which may indicate shifts in your mental state or personal growth.
4. **Goal tracking**: AI can monitor your progress toward stated goals and offer encouragement or suggestions for improvement.
5. **Relationship insights**: Examine how you write about different people in your life to gain insight into your social dynamics.

Example AI analysis:

"Based on your posts over the past month, you mention work-related stress 43% more often than in previous months. However, posts discussing your new meditation practice correlate with a 20% increase in positive sentiment words. You may want to consider expanding your mindfulness practice to help you manage work stress."

PRIVACY AND SECURITY CONCERNS WITH AI-AUGMENTED JOURNALING

As we entrust our private thoughts to AI systems, we need to be vigilant about data security:

1. **End-to-end encryption**: Make sure any app you use encrypts your data both in transit and at rest.
2. **Local processing**: Prefer apps that process your data on the device rather than sending it to cloud servers.
3. **Data ownership**: Read the terms of service carefully to understand who owns the data generated from your input.
4. **Deletion rights**: Confirm that you have the ability to permanently delete your data from the service.
5. **Third-party sharing**: Be wary of apps that share your data with third parties, even in an anonymized form.

Example Reflection:

"I'm torn between the insights AI analytics could provide and my desire for absolute privacy. Can I really bare my soul knowing that my words could be processed by algorithms? Isn't any digital diary a compromise of perfect privacy? I need to research the security measures of these apps more thoroughly before I decide."

THE FUTURE OF AI IN JOURNALING: PREDICTIONS AND POSSIBILITIES

As AI technology continues to advance, we can expect even more sophisticated integrations with journaling:

1. Predictive journaling: AI could suggest entire entries based on your past writing and current context, which you could then edit and refine.
2. Immersive experiences: Virtual or augmented reality journaling environments tailored by AI to enhance your reflective state.
3. Multimodal analysis: AI could integrate data from wearables, environmental sensors, and your writing to provide holistic insights into your well-being.
4. AI therapist integration: Your journaling app could offer AI-

driven therapeutic interventions based on the content of your entries.
5. Collective insights: Anonymized data from millions of journals could be analyzed to identify societal trends and collective emotional states.

BALANCING AUTHENTIC SELF-EXPRESSION WITH AI SUPPORT

As we navigate this new terrain, maintaining authenticity in our journaling practice will be paramount:

1. **Use AI as a tool, not a crutch**: Let it enhance your writing, not replace your voice.
2. Practice AI-free journaling: Practice traditional journaling regularly to maintain your unassisted writing skills.
3. **Critically engage with AI suggestions**: Question and evaluate the input you receive, rather than accepting it unthinkingly.
4. **Personalize your AI**: Take time to "train" your AI assistant to better understand your unique voice and preferences.
5. **Reflect on the process**: Journal regularly about your experience using AI in your practice. How does it affect your self-expression?

EXERCISES FOR EXPLORING YOUR RELATIONSHIP WITH AI IN PERSONAL WRITING

1. **AI Dialogue**: Have a written conversation with an AI about your journaling practice. Reflect on how it feels to discuss personal matters with an artificial entity.
2. **Comparative Analysis**: Write two entries on the same topic, one with AI assistance and one without. Compare the results and your experience writing each one.

3. **Future Visioning**: Imagine and describe your ideal AI journaling assistant. What features would it have? What ethical guidelines would govern its operation?
4. **AI-generated self-portrait:** Have an AI analyze your past entries and generate a description of you. Think about its accuracy and what it might reveal about how you present yourself in writing.

DEVELOPING CRITICAL THINKING SKILLS FOR THE AI AGE

As AI becomes more integrated into our personal practices, honing our critical thinking skills will be critical:

1. **Question assumptions**: Regularly question the assumptions underlying AI suggestions or analyses.
2. **Seek diverse perspectives**: Use AI to expose you to viewpoints different from your own, but always engage with them critically.
3. **Understand AI limitations**: Understand the current capabilities and limitations of AI to maintain realistic expectations.
4. **Practice metacognition**: Reflect on your own thought processes and how they might be affected by AI interactions.
5. **Ethical reasoning**: Regularly consider the ethical implications of your AI use and be prepared to adjust your practices accordingly.

CREATING GUIDELINES FOR ETHICAL AI USE IN YOUR JOURNALING PRACTICE

Establish personal guidelines to ensure that your AI-enhanced journaling is consistent with your values:

1. **Define your red lines**: Identify aspects of your practice that you want to keep AI-free.

2. **Establish a review process**: Regularly assess the impact of AI on your journals and be prepared to adjust your use.
3. **Set standards for transparency**: Choose apps that are clear about their AI use and data practices.
4. **Create a data management plan**: Decide how you'll store, back up, and eventually dispose of your AI-enhanced journal entries.
5. **Commit to ongoing education:** Commit to staying informed about AI developments and their potential impact on personal writing.

Example policy:

"I will use AI for prompts and light editing suggestions, but all substantive content will come from me. I will review each AI suggestion and make a conscious decision to accept or reject it. I will not use AI for entries that deal with my deepest emotions or most private experiences. I will export and locally save all my entries monthly and review my use of AI quarterly."

CONCLUSION: NAVIGATING THE AI-ENHANCED JOURNALING LANDSCAPE

As we stand at the intersection of personal reflection and artificial intelligence, we face both unprecedented opportunities and complex challenges. AI has the potential to deepen our self-understanding, enhance our creativity, and provide insights we might never achieve alone. But it also raises profound questions about the nature of self-expression, the sanctity of our inner thoughts, and the role of technology in our most personal practices.

Your journal remains, as always, a space for exploration and growth. As you navigate this new terrain, let your curiosity guide you, but temper it with critical thinking and a strong ethical framework. Experiment with AI tools, think deeply about their implications, and always prioritize your authentic voice and personal privacy.

The future of journaling is unfolding before us, shaped by the ever-evolving dance between human introspection and artificial intelligence. By engaging thoughtfully with these new technologies, we can harness their power while preserving the deeply human core of our journaling practice.

Remember, the most powerful insights will always come from within. AI can be a remarkable tool, but it's your unique experiences, emotions, and reflections that truly bring your journal to life. Keep writing, keep questioning, and keep growing - with or without AI as your journey companion.

FIFTEEN
THE JOURNEY OF JOURNALING – A REFLECTION

The blank page beckons, a silent invitation to explore the depths of your mind and soul. Throughout this book, we've traversed the rich landscape of journaling, discovering its myriad forms and profound effects. Let's pause now to reflect on our journey.

We began by exploring the fundamental power of putting pen to paper-or fingers to keyboard. The simple act of journaling opens doors to self-discovery, creativity, and personal growth. It's a practice as old as writing itself, yet forever relevant.

Your journaling toolkit, we discovered, is deeply personal. From the tactile pleasure of a leather-bound notebook to the convenience of digital apps, your choice of medium shapes your experience. Remember, the best tool is the one you use consistently.

As we delved into techniques, we explored the art of reflection, the power of stream-of-consciousness writing, and the structure of prompted entries. Each method offers a unique path to insight, allowing you to tailor your practice to your needs and moods.

Creativity flourishes within the pages of a journal. We have explored how to unleash your artistic self by combining words with visual elements to create a rich, multidimensional record of your inner world.

Structure has its place, too. We explored how bullet journaling and other organized approaches can transform your journal into a powerful tool for productivity and goal-setting.

In the digital age, we looked at the opportunities and challenges of online journaling. From apps to AI assistants, technology offers new frontiers for self-expression - but also raises important questions about privacy and authenticity.

Mindfulness and journaling, we found, have a powerful synergy. By bringing present-moment awareness to your writing practice, you deepen both your self-understanding and your capacity for peace.

We delved into the deeply personal realm of journaling for mental health, exploring how writing can help manage anxiety, depression, and stress. Your journal becomes a trusted confidant and a tool for emotional regulation.

For those facing chronic illness, we discovered how journaling can be a lifeline-a way to track symptoms, process emotions, and maintain a sense of self in the midst of health challenges.

We ventured into the world of activism, exploring how journals can document social movements and catalyze personal and collective change. Their words, we learned, have the power to shape history.

Environmental consciousness found its place in our exploration. Eco-journaling connects us deeply to the natural world, promoting sustainable practices and a heightened sense of our place within the ecosystem.

Finally, we explored the emerging frontier of AI in journaling. The possibilities are both exciting and unsettling, prompting us to consider what it means to truly express ourselves in a technologically augmented world.

Throughout these chapters, one truth has remained constant: journaling is a deeply personal practice that evolves with you. It's a mirror that reflects your growth, a canvas for your dreams, and a companion on life's winding path.

As you continue your journaling journey, remember that there's no "right" way to do it. Experiment, explore, and find what resonates with you. Some days the words will flow effortlessly. Other days, you'll struggle to write a single line. Both experiences are valuable, part of the beautiful complexity of engaging with your inner world.

Your journal is a testament to your life - messy, imperfect, and utterly unique. It's a space where you can be fully, unabashedly yourself. So keep writing, keep reflecting, keep growing. The blank page awaits, ready to receive whatever you bring to it. Your story is still unfolding, one entry at a time.

APPENDIX A: JOURNALING PROMPTS FOR EVERY OCCASION

Inspirational writing prompts: Great for getting your pen moving and exploring new areas of self-reflection. Here are some prompts, grouped by topic, to get you started-whether you're journaling your day, exploring your emotions, or setting goals.

DAILY REFLECTION PROMPTS

1. What was the highlight of my day, and why?
2. What was challenging for me today and how did I deal with it?
3. For what am I most grateful today?
4. How did I contribute to someone else's happiness today?
5. What is one thing I learnt today?
6. How did I look after myself today?
7. What feelings have I had today, and what was the cause of them?
8. How can I make tomorrow better than today?

SELF-DISCOVERY PROMPTS

1. Who am I at my core, and what do I stand for?
2. What are my largest aspirations, and what can I do to make them happen?
3. What is my personal definition of success and am I living it?
4. How are my limiting beliefs holding me back, and what can I do to change how I view the world?
5. What is my vision of an ideal life, and what steps can I take to get one step closer to that?
6. What are my greatest strengths, and how might I utilize them even better?
7. What behaviors or habits would I want to change? Why?
8. What is self-love to me, and how can I best practice it daily?

EMOTIONAL DISCOVERY PROMPTS

1. What emotions have I been avoiding and why?
2. Generally, how do I react to stress, and how can I do it better?
3. What fears are currently holding me back, and how can I face them?
4. Show love and affection, and how does it affect your relationships?
5. Which experiences contributed to forming my present emotional state?
6. How do I handle anger, and what are healthier ways to express it?
7. What is forgiveness and who has hurt me, including myself, that I need to forgive?
8. How do I deal with my sadness and what do I turn to for solace during my own difficult times?

GOAL-SETTING PROMPTS

1. What are my top three goals for the upcoming year, and what makes them so important to me?
2. What are some challenges that I could face in order to achieve these goals, and how might I overcome them?
3. What daily habits can I form that will keep my goals alive?
4. How will the accomplishment of these goals improve my life?
5. Who could help me achieve my goals, and how might I ask for their assistance?
6. Which are the skills or knowledge that I need to develop to be able to accomplish what I want to?
7. How will I celebrate when I reach my goals?
8. What smaller milestones can I set to track my progress toward my goals?

CREATIVE EXPLORATION PROMPTS

1. What exactly is creativity to me and how do I personally express it?
2. If I could create anything without limitation, what would it be?
3. What do I get the most inspired by, and how can I use it for my creative process?
4. What place does failure have in my journey of creativity, and how can I learn to embrace it?
5. How do I get over creative blocks, and what are the techniques that I could use if I got stuck?
6. On a lighter note, what is/are my favorite creative outlet and how does it/these bring me joy?
7. Who is the artist whose work I would most like to collaborate with, both living and dead?
8. What is the message I desire to share through my creativity?

PROMPTS FOR FUTURE VISION

1. Where do I see myself in five years, and what am I doing to get there?
2. What impact or legacy do I want to leave behind, and what can I start building on that today?
3. How do I see my perfect day in the future, and how do I make that the reality?
4. Which personal qualities do I want bringing out or enhancing in the next few years?
5. How do I want my relationships to evolve over time, and what can I do to nurture them?
6. What kind of new experiences do I want, and how can I manifest a way to bring those opportunities to myself?
7. How can I help my community, or even the world, in some great way?
8. What would I say to my future self, and what advice would I give?

APPENDIX B: RESOURCES AND FURTHER READING

To delve deeper into your journaling practice, learn new skills, or simply get inspiration, these books, articles, and resources can be helpful in journaling and personal development.

BOOKS ABOUT JOURNALING

1. **The Artist's Way by Julia Cameron** – Classic book on creativity and an introduction to Morning Pages, a powerful daily writing practice.
2. **Writing Down Your Soul by Janet Conner**: Using your journal as a spiritual practice into deeper layers of self-awareness.
3. **Kathleen Adams, "Journal to the Self*** - Offers a huge breadth of journaling techniques and exercises that foster personal growth and creative expression.
4. **"The Bullet Journal Method" by Ryder Carroll**: The author reviews the method of organizing one's life through Bullet Journals.

5. **Meera Lee Patel, "Start Where You Are: A Journal for Self-Exploration":** A beautiful book with exercises and prompts to determine who you are.
6. **"The Power of Now Journal" by Eckhart Tolle** – One of those companion volumes to Tolle's best-selling book, to encourage mindfulness and present-moment awareness through writing.

ARTICLES ABOUT JOURNALING

1. **The Science Behind Journaling: How Writing Your Emotions Can Be Good for Your Health** – Discusses research that indicates ways in which journaling can be supportive for mental and physical health.
2. **"How to Start Journaling for Self-Improvement":** A step-by-step guide for the use of journaling to be better by the beginner.
3. **"Why You Should Keep a Journal and How to Start"**- Tips for beginning and keeping a journal, and why you would DEVOTE TIME TO IT.
4. **"The Power of Gratitude Journaling"** - In this talk, you will learn how gratitude journaling will increase well-being and a positive mentality.

ONLINE JOURNALING COMMUNITIES

1. **The International Association for Journal Writing (IAJW)** – Offers resource, classes, and community for journal writers committed to journal writing.
2. **Reddit's r/Journaling** – An active online community where journalers share tips, prompts, and experiences.
3. **Pen & Paper Journaling Community on Facebook**: A Facebook community for pen and paper journaling, where inspiration and support are given.

4. **Bullet Journalists on Instagram**: Follow hashtags like #bullet journal and #bujo for creative inspiration and ideas from the Bullet Journaling community.

JOURNALING SUPPLIES

1. **Leuchtturm1917 Notebooks**: With the strength and versatility that has made these notebooks a popular choice for journalers, it is useful for both traditional and Bullet Journaling.
2. **Moleskine Notebooks** – Another favorite for all journalers: the classic in style with many different sizes and formats.
3. **Pilot G2 Gel Pens** – These pens are every journaler's favorite, as they write nice and smooth; with rich ink, it would be just a bliss.
4. Washi Tape – Used to decorate journal pages; it's tape in all sorts of colors and patterns.
5. **Tombow Dual Brush Pens** – Flexible pens with brush tips for journaling creativity and hand lettering.

These will indeed provide a wealth of information and inspiration that shall deepen the journaling practice, explore new techniques, and connect with others of like passion in writing and personal growth.

APPENDIX C: DIGITAL TOOLS AND APPLICATIONS FOR JOURNALING

Here are some of the top tools and apps in the digital realm to supplement traditional practice with, or with which to do digital journaling.

DIGITAL JOURNALING APPS

1. **Day One**

Platform: iOS, Android, and macOS

Features: Automatic metadata: location, weather, and activity Photo and video integration End-to-end encryption Multiple journals Tagging Search.

Best For: Extensive journaling, with a focus on privacy and multimedia integration

2. **Journey**

Platforms: iOS, Android, macOS, Windows, Web

Features: Daily Prompts, Mood tracking, Google Drive integration, reminders for journaling, and support for cloud sync on all devices.

Best For: Journaling; focusing on high-quality reflection and habit-building every day.

3. **Penzu**

Platforms: iOS, Android, Web

Features: All the notes are military-grade encrypted, custom journal cover, upload photos, email reminders, and search.

Best For: Secure journaling with the emphasis on privacy.

4. **Notion**

Platforms: iOS, Android, macOS, Windows, Web

Features: Templates that a user can configure, databases, tagging, multimedia, and various collaboration features.

Best For: Freeform journaling mixed with task management and project planning.

5. **Microsoft OneNote**

Platforms: iOS, Android, macOS, Windows, Web

Features: Free-form note-taking, ink support, multimedia integration, and section and page organization; also, it allows cloud synchronization with OneDrive.

Best For: Free-form journaling with strong multimedia and organizational capabilities.

NOTE-TAKING AND WRITING APPS

1. **Evernote**

Platforms: iOS, Android, macOS, Windows, Web

Features: Note-seizing, task managing, scanning of documents, clipping from the web, synchronizing with the cloud, and organization.

Best for: Integrated note-taking and journaling with a big organizational feature set

2. **Bear**

Platforms: iOS, macOS

Features: Support for markdowns, tagging, the ability to integrate images in line, linking of notes crosswise, theming,.

Good for: Minimalist, distraction-free writing with advanced formatting options

3. **Google Keep**

Platforms: iOS, Android, Web

Features: Note-taking, check-list making, reminder setting, colour-coded organization, and integration.

Best For: Fast, easy note-taking with Cloud sync and reminders.

4. **Scrivener**

Platforms: Mac OS, Windows, Linux

Features: Long document support, organization tools, corkboard view, integration for research, export.

Best For: Writing journals, especially for writers needing extensive writing and project management support.

MIND MAPPING AND BRAINSTORMING TOOLS

1. MindMeister

Platforms: iOS, Android, Web

Features: Collaboration on mind maps, cloud storage, presentation mode, export.

Best For: Visual thinkers who use mind maps to organize their thoughts and ideas.

3. XMind

Platforms: iOS, Android, macOS, Windows, Linux

Features: Brainstorming tools for mind mapping, Gantt charts, and flowcharts; export type.

Best For: Detail-packed and structured visual brainstorming.

3. Milanote

Platforms: Web, iOS

Features: Visual boards, drag-and-drop interface, taking notes on the platform, adding images and links, collaboration.

Best For: Creative professionals looking to combine journaling with visual project planning.

Considering this, digital tools and apps present features supporting many styles of journaling and just as many needs. Whether you are looking for a simple app with which to jot down ideas, or if you need a suite of applications with which to keep your daily life in order, digital tools offer a significant upgrade to your practice.

APPENDIX D: SAMPLE JOURNAL ENTRIES

Following are a few example journal entries for beginners or for those seeking inspiration, showing different journaling techniques and styles.

DAILY REFLECTION ENTRY

Date: September 5, 2024

Today Highlights:

It has been a good day, though. By far, the best thing was the walk by the lake this morning. It was cool, a zephyr, and the water was so pacified. I felt such a deep sense of peace and connection to nature. It was a reminder of most times, how important it is to take time for myself—even when life gets busy.

Challenges:

Work was a bit stressing, though, especially during the meeting held in the afternoon. I felt frustrated because my suggestions were not taken in the spirit, nevertheless, I kept my cool and focused. I still have to work on being more assertive without showing aggressiveness.

Gratitude:

On the bright side, grateful for the beautiful weather and the chance to walk by the lake.

Grateful for the support of my counterpart, Sarah, who helped me maneuver through the meeting.

Grateful for the delicious dinner I cooked tonight—cooking proves an actual source of joy for me.

Tomorrow's Intentions:

Focus on being positive and finding little moments of joy throughout the day tomorrow. Prepare more thoroughly for the meetings so that I can present my ideas with confidence.

REFLECTIVE ENTRY

Date: March 15, 2024

Topic: Facing Fear Lately

I have been thinking a lot about fear—how it manifests in my life and how it paralyzes me. My greatest fear has been the fear of failure. I have always been afraid that I would not want to take risks because I would not want to be caught making a mistake or looking silly. But I am beginning to notice that this fear is keeping me away from growth and experiences. I just bumped into this quote today that really struck: "What would you do if you weren't afraid?" This quote brought lights to all the opportunities that I let bypass my own hands just because I was afraid. I hope if I give myself more opportunities in life, let it be a little structured around risks—personal failures as a continuous part of the learning process. And I would like to start by taking some small steps out of my comfort zone. They don't have to be major; little steps that prod me into growth will do. I'll make a list of things I have been avoiding because of fear and start to attempt them one by one. I know that it won't but I'm all set to the challenge covering what's on the other side.

CREATIVE ENTRY

Date: June 22, 2024

Title: The Garden of My Mind

My thoughts come up in the garden of my mind, without a care, wild like flowers, bold in color, completely unrestricted in energy—there is one this way to the sun, and that. Some of them are bold and vivid, stretching for the sun with all their might, but others are delicate, hiding from the sun, and they wait for that perfect moment to be tenderly unveiled. Of course, there are the weeds, too—the doubts and fears that threaten the very life from the flowers. But I'm learning to tend it, to weed and water the blooms. That's not always easy, and at times, I question if I'm doing it right. But then of course, I remember that perfection doesn't make natural beauty. Today, I sow seeds of hope and possibility, watering each one with kindness and patience and with the faith that they will sprout when the time is right. I learn to trust the process of believing in the beauty of what I have created, even when I do not yet see.

GOAL-SETTING ENTRY

Date: January 1, 2024

Goal: Run a Half-Marathon

I have set myself a big goal for this year: I am going to be able to run a half marathon. This is something I have always wanted to do but never thought I could do. I have been running for quite a long time, but I have never pushed myself further than a few miles. This year, I want to see what I am made of:

Action Steps

1. **Develop a training plan**: I will first search online for training plans for beginners and select one that best fits my schedule.
2. **Set mini-goals**: I will set smaller goals and break down the training into smaller, easier-to-understand steps—such as increasing my mileage in a week's time and participating in shorter races.]
3. **Hold yourself accountabl**e: I'm going to keep this journal as a way to track my progress and be sure to give myself bi-weekly check-ins. I may even find a running group or a running buddy to keep me accountable.
4. **Nutrition focus**: I'll make sure that I fuel with the correct foods to match my training.
5. **Celebrate progress**: For every small milestone that I hit, be it running my first 5 kilometers or reaching for that new personal best, I will take a moment to congratulate myself by knowing how hard I have worked and how far I have come. This is a goal that I know will be challenging, but at the same time, it will be interesting to see how far I can go. I am ready to invest the effort and prove to myself that I really can do something that I earlier thought was impossible.

These sample journal entries give an insight into the wide variety of journaling styles and techniques. From boiling your reflections down to what has passed in the day, emerging out of feelings, into goal setting, or activating your creativity, these examples can serve you in inspiration for your own journal writing practice. Keep in mind that there is no right or wrong way to journal; your entries are very private and express your own thoughts and feelings.

ABOUT THE AUTHOR

Richard French, a pioneering technology leader and entrepreneur, brings his wealth of experience in innovation and personal growth to the realm of journaling. As a driving force behind several successful technology companies, Richard has consistently demonstrated the power of self-reflection and clear goal-setting in achieving remarkable business transformations.

With a career spanning software, AI, and global business leadership, Richard has guided organizations from startup stage to multi-million dollar enterprises. His philosophy that "people work with us, not for us" underlies his approach to personal development and team building.

A mathematics graduate and GT race car driver, Richard combines analytical thinking with a passion for pushing boundaries. In "The Art of Journaling," he applies his unique perspective on goal achievement and self-expression, offering readers a roadmap to personal transformation drawn from his experiences in the fast-paced worlds of technology and motorsports.

Richard's insights, honed through years of leading innovation and speaking at industry conferences, now guide readers on their journey of self-discovery through the power of journaling.

www.ingramcontent.com/pod-product-compliance
Lightning Source LLC
Chambersburg PA
CBHW060530130626
46553CB00002B/698